Slow Cooker Favorites

VEGETARIAN

150+ EASY, DELICIOUS SLOW COOKER RECIPES,
from Stuffed Peppers and Scalloped Potatoes to Simple Ratatouille

Adams Media
New York London Toronto Sydney New Delhi

Adams Media
An Imprint of Simon & Schuster, Inc.
57 Littlefield Street
Avon, Massachusetts 02322

First Adams Media trade paperback edition JANUARY 2018

ADAMS MEDIA and colophon are trademarks of Simon and Schuster.

For information about special discounts for bulk purchases, please contact Simon & Schuster Special Sales at 1-866-506-1949 or business@simonandschuster.com.

The Simon & Schuster Speakers Bureau can bring authors to your live event. For more information or to book an event contact the Simon & Schuster Speakers Bureau at 1-866-248-3049 or visit our website at www.simonspeakers.com.

Interior design by Katrina Machado

Manufactured in the United States of America

10 9 8 7 6 5 4 3 2 1

LCC TX827 (ebook) | LCC TX827 .S55274 2018 (print) | DDC 641.5/884--dc23
LC record available at https://lccn.loc.gov/2017035853

ISBN 978-1-5072-0640-9
ISBN 978-1-5072-0641-6 (ebook)

Contains material adapted from the following titles published by Adams Media, an Imprint of Simon & Schuster, Inc.: *The Everything® Vegan Slow Cooker Cookbook* by Amy Snyder and Justin Snyder, copyright © 2012, ISBN 978-1-4405-4407-1, and *The Everything® Vegetarian Slow Cooker Cookbook* by Amy Snyder and Justin Snyder, copyright © 2012, ISBN 978-1-4405-2858-3.

Library of Congress Cataloging-in-Publication Data
Adams Media, firm.
Slow cooker favorites: vegetarian.
Avon, Massachusetts: Adams Media, 2018.
Series: Slow Cooker Favorites.
Includes index.
LCCN 2017035853 (print) | LCCN 2017042841 (ebook) | ISBN 9781507206409 (pb) | ISBN 9781507206416 (ebook)
LCSH: Electric cooking, Slow. | Vegetarian cooking. | LCGFT: Cookbooks.

Contents

Introduction

Are you sick of cleaning up a mountain of dirty dishes? Looking to serve a crowd? Does the simple act of eating a home-cooked meal seem like a luxury?

If this sounds familiar, it's time for you to plug in your slow cooker and make a hot meal a priority—not a chore.

With a slow cooker you can create everything from appetizers to soups and stews to flavorful entrées, and you don't have to worry about spending hours—or much time at all—in the kitchen. Just drop in your ingredients, turn on the slow cooker, and you're out the door with a delicious dinner guaranteed to greet you when you get home.

In *Slow Cooker Favorites: Vegetarian* you'll find more than 150 vegetarian slow cooker recipes that make dinnertime easy, inexpensive, and incredibly versatile. These flavor-packed dishes come from a variety of cuisines—Mediterranean, Italian, Asian, and Indian—and even include a number of American favorites like Tofu Pepper Steak, Seitan Pot Pie, and Bananas Foster. You'll also find a chapter that gives you the rundown on how to use, clean, and store your slow cooker and information on how to customize your recipes once you get the hang of using this appliance.

So whether you're craving French Onion Soup, Gingered Sweet Potatoes, Vegan Ropa Vieja, or just some good old Mock Meatloaf, with *Slow Cooker Favorites: Vegetarian* you'll always know what's for dinner.

CHAPTER 1

Slow Cooker Basics

So you know you want to use a slow cooker and you're excited to use the recipes in this book to whip up delicious vegetarian meals. But, where do you start? In this chapter, you'll learn everything you need to know to choose, cook with, clean, and store your slow cooker. In addition, you'll find some basic techniques for using this appliance as well as some info on the methods and terminology used in the book to make cooking with your slow cooker as easy as possible. Let's get cooking!

What Slow Cooker Equipment Should You Buy?

Maybe you've gone to buy a slow cooker and were intimidated by all the options. With so many different styles from which to choose, how do you pick the one that's right for you?

There are small 1-quart versions that are perfect for hot-dip appetizers and large 8-quart models that make enough stew for a large family. There are versions with automatic timers and warming settings. Some have removable crockery inserts, while others have the crock built into the device.

The first thing you need to do is take a look at how you'll be using the device. Are you routinely gone for more than nine hours during the day? If so, you might want to consider the automatic timer and warming functions because even a slow cooker can overcook some food. Do you want to make entire meals? The two-compartment model would provide more options. If you don't like to spend a lot of time washing pots and pans, consider a slow cooker with a removable crockery insert. These can be cleaned in the dishwasher, while self-contained units must be sponge cleaned. The good news is that a slow cooker remains a slow cooker. It's a relatively simple device that's hard to use incorrectly.

If you are lucky enough to plan your purchase of a slow cooker, define what you will be using it for. Do you have more than four people in your family? If so, you might want to go with a 6-quart or even an 8-quart version. Someone who does a lot of entertaining or likes to freeze leftovers might want the larger version. Many of the recipes throughout this book call for either a 4- or a 6-quart slow cooker, so keep that in mind while choosing your appliance. Once you decide what type of slow cooker to buy, you'll need to figure out how to use it. Read on...

How to Use Your Slow Cooker

Today's slow cookers usually have two settings—high and low. The low setting is equivalent to about 200°F at its highest, while the high setting gets up to about 300°F. However, the reason they are listed as high and low is because the actual degrees don't matter. Since the food heats indirectly, absorbing the heat from the crockery, it will cook the same way within a 50-degree temperature range.

Slow cookers heat up slowly, usually taking two to three hours to get up to their highest temperature. This ensures that the food retains its nutrients while also preventing scorching or burning. It's also the reason you don't need to be home while the meal cooks. When your slow cooker is on, resist the urge to lift the cover to view, smell, or stir the contents. Every time you lift the cover of the slow cooker, valuable steam escapes, reducing the internal temperature several degrees. This steam that the slow cooker creates is an important factor in creating those marvelous flavors—foods are cooked in their own steam, literally infusing the flavor back in through the cooking process. This keeps the food moist and works to tenderize even the most stubborn vegetables. Every time you lift the cover, plan to add at least twenty minutes to your cooking time.

Slow Cooker Suggestions

The heating elements for a slow cooker are across the bottom of the slow cooker and up the sides. Until you become very familiar with the quirks of your slow cooker, cooking on low is the safest bet for ensuring the food turns out the way you want it.

Even the most inexperienced cook can quickly master slow cooker recipes. Just keep the following things in mind:

- Cut vegetables to the same size to ensure even cooking in soups and stews.
- Place slow-cooking items such as hard vegetables—rutabagas, turnips, potatoes—on the bottom of the slow cooker.
- Slow cooker recipes don't like water. Because the food is infused with steam, very little water escapes. When converting a recipe from a regular cookbook, use about half the water and add more during the last hour of the cooking cycle if necessary.

- Most traditional slow cooker recipes take seven to nine hours on the low setting. The high setting takes about half that time but doesn't tenderize the ingredients as much.
- Spices and aromatic vegetables have different characteristics when slow cooked. Some, such as green peppers and bay leaves, increase in intensity when slow cooked. Others, such as onions and cinnamon, tend to lose flavor over the long cooking process. Most slow cooker recipes reflect this difference, although you may have to adjust for your own tastes.
- When cooking traditional slow cooker meals such as soups and stews, make sure the slow cooker is at least half full and the food does not extend beyond 1" below the top. This ensures even cooking.
- Don't thaw food in the slow cooker. While it may seem a natural use, frozen food actually heats up too slowly to effectively prevent bacterial growth when in a slow cooker. It's better to thaw food overnight in a refrigerator or use the microwave.

With these things in mind, you'll be a slow cooker professional before you know it.

How to Care for Your Slow Cooker

Slow cookers are very simple appliances. However, they do need some special care. If you follow these rules, your slow cooker will produce healthy meals for many years:

- Never, never, never immerse the slow cooker in water. If it's plugged in at the time, you could receive a shock. If it isn't plugged in, you could damage the heating element.
- Always check for nicks or cuts in the electrical cord before plugging it into the outlet. This is especially important because you may be leaving the slow cooker on for several hours with no one in the home.
- Parts of the slow cooker can be cleaned in a dishwasher. If you have a removable crockery core, place it on the bottom rack. If you have a plastic cover, be sure to place it in the top rack of the dishwasher so

it doesn't warp. If the crockery container isn't removable, simply use a soft cloth or sponge to wash it out. Always use a damp cloth to wash the metal housing.

- Remove baked-on food from the crockery container with a nonabrasive cleaner and a damp sponge. Do not scrub with abrasives, as these can scratch the crock, creating areas for bacteria to reside.

Be sure to follow all of these rules to guarantee your slow cooker will both last for many years and perform at maximum potential with each use.

Slow Cooker Suggestions

Cooking with a slow cooker becomes even easier when you use slow cooker liners. The liners are made of food-safe, heat-resistant nylon. They also make slow cooker cleanup fast and easy, because you simply place the liner in the slow cooker crock, add the ingredients, cook according to the recipe instructions, throw the liner away when you're done, and then wipe down the slow cooker and wash the lid.

What Else Do You Need to Know?

So now you know how to buy, cook with, and clean your slow cooker. Now let's take a look at what else you need to know to successfully make the deliciously easy meals found throughout the following recipes.

Learn Some Cooking Terms

Throughout this book, you'll encounter cooking terms usually associated with other methods of cooking. While the slow cooker does provide an easy way to cook foods, there are simple tricks you can use to let your slow cooker mimic those other methods. Cooking method terms you'll find in this book include the following:

- **Baking** usually involves putting the food that's in a baking pan or ovenproof casserole dish in a preheated oven; the food cooks by being surrounded by the hot, dry air of your oven. (In the case of a convection oven, it cooks by being surrounded by circulating hot, dry air.) In the slow cooker, food can be steam-baked in the cooker itself, or you can mimic the effect of baking at a low oven temperature by putting the food in a baking dish and resting that dish on a cooking insert or rack.

- **Braising** usually starts by browning vegetables in a skillet on top of the stove and then putting the vegetables with a small amount of liquid in a pan with a lid or covering and slowly cooking them. Braising can take place on the stovetop, in the oven, or in a slow cooker. The slow-cooking process tenderizes the vegetables. Incidentally, the liquid that's in the pan after you've braised vegetables often can be used to make a flavorful sauce or gravy.
- **Sautéing** is the method of quickly cooking small or thin pieces of food in some oil or butter that has been brought to temperature in a sauté pan over medium to medium-high heat. Alternatively, you can sauté in a good-quality nonstick pan without using added fat; instead use a little broth, nonstick cooking spray, or water in place of the oil or butter. As mentioned later in this chapter, another alternative is to steam-sauté food in the microwave.
- **Stewing** is similar to braising in that food is slowly cooked in a liquid; however, stewing involves a larger liquid-to-food ratio. In other words, you use far more liquid when you're stewing food. It is the method often associated with recipes for the slow cooker. Not surprising, this method is most often used to make stew.

Make Each Dish Your Own

Throughout this book you'll find suggestions for how you can take shortcuts or add a bit of additional personality to a dish without compromising the recipe. Straying from the recipe may seem scary at first, but once you understand the logic behind such shortcuts, you'll begin to look at them as alternative measures rather than total improvisations. Before you know it, you'll be adding a little bit of this and a little bit of that with the best of them. For example:

- **Use broth bases or homemade broth:** Use of a broth base or homemade broth lets you eliminate the need to sauté vegetables. In addition, broth bases can be made double strength, which saves you the time of reducing broth and you avoid that briny, overly salty taste associated with bouillon cubes. Bases also take up less storage space. It usually only takes ¾ to 1 teaspoon of broth mixed together with a cup of water to make 1 cup of broth. A 16-ounce container of base, for example, is enough to make 6 gallons of broth.

- **Use a microwave-safe measuring cup:** Rather than dirtying a microwave-safe bowl and a measuring cup, planning the steps so that you add the ingredients to a microwave-safe measuring cup means you can use it to sauté or steam onions or other vegetables called for in the recipe. This makes it easier to pour the results into the slow cooker and you end up with fewer dishes to wash.

- **Steam-sauté vegetables in the microwave:** Sautéing vegetables in the microwave has the added advantage of using less oil than it would take to sauté them in a pan. Or you can compromise further and eliminate the oil entirely and substitute broth if you prefer. Just because a recipe suggests sautéing the onions in a nonstick skillet doesn't mean that you can't use the alternative microwave method, or vice versa. Use the method that is most convenient for you. On the other hand, skipping other steps, like sautéing onion, carrot, celery, or bell pepper before you add them to the slow cooker, won't ruin the taste of the food; you'll just end up with a dish that tastes good instead of great. When time is an issue, there may be times when good is good enough. And that's okay.

- **Take advantage of ways to enhance or correct the flavor:** Like salt, a little bit of sugar can act as a flavor enhancer. The sweetness of sugar, honey, applesauce, or jelly can also be used to help tame an overly hot spicy dish or curry. Just start out adding a little bit at a time; you want to adjust the flavor without ending up with a dish with a cloying result.

- **Use fresh herbs:** There are other times you may need to adjust some of the recipe instructions. For example, if you have fresh herbs on hand, it's almost always better to use those instead of dried seasoning; however, if you substitute fresh herbs, don't add them until near the end of the cooking time. Also keep in mind that you need to use three times the amount called for in the recipe. In other words, if the recipe specifies 1 teaspoon of dried thyme, you'd add 1 tablespoon (3 teaspoons) of fresh thyme.

- **Use frozen, not fresh:** If you're using frozen vegetables to replace the fresh vegetables called for in the recipe, chances are you can add them straight from the freezer to the slow cooker and not greatly affect the cooking time.

Again, if you're nervous or just aren't comfortable cooking with a slow cooker yet, don't worry. Follow the recipes in this book, learn what you like and what you don't like, and then take the next step. The possibilities are endless!

CHAPTER 2

Breakfasts

Tofu Frittata

2 tablespoons olive oil

1 cup peeled and diced red potatoes

1/2 medium onion, diced

1/2 cup diced red pepper

1/2 cup diced green pepper

1 teaspoon minced jalapeño

1 clove garlic, minced

1/4 cup chopped fresh parsley

1 (16-ounce) package firm tofu

1/2 cup unsweetened soymilk

4 teaspoons cornstarch

2 tablespoons nutritional yeast

1 teaspoon ground mustard

1/2 teaspoon turmeric

1 teaspoon salt

1/4 teaspoon black pepper

1. Add the oil to a sauté pan and sauté the potatoes, onions, peppers, jalapeño, and garlic on medium-high heat for 5–10 minutes. Place the mixture in a 4-quart slow cooker.

2. Meanwhile, in a blender or food processor, combine the rest of the ingredients until smooth, then pour the mixture into the slow cooker with the potatoes.

3. Cover and cook on high heat for 4 hours, or until the frittata has firmed.

Slow Cooker Suggestions

To shorten the preparation time for this meal while keeping all of the flavors, try making this dish into a scramble by preparing the entire recipe in the slow cooker. Skip the step of blending the tofu and omit the cornstarch. Add remaining ingredients, breaking apart tofu as you stir, and sauté until cooked through.

Sunrise Tofu Scramble

SERVES 4

1 (16-ounce) package firm tofu, drained and crumbled

½ cup broccoli florets, chopped

½ cup button mushrooms, sliced

2 tablespoons olive oil

2 teaspoons turmeric

1 teaspoon cumin

¼ teaspoon garlic powder

⅛ teaspoon red pepper flakes

2 cloves garlic, minced

1 teaspoon salt

¼ teaspoon black pepper

½ cup diced tomatoes

1 lemon, juiced

2 tablespoons chopped fresh parsley

1. Add the tofu, broccoli, mushrooms, oil, turmeric, cumin, garlic powder, red pepper flakes, garlic, salt, and black pepper to a 4-quart slow cooker.
2. Cover and cook on low heat for 4 hours.
3. Add the tomatoes, lemon juice, and parsley to the scramble and serve.

Cheese Grits

SERVES 4

2 cups stone-ground grits

6 cups water

2 tablespoons butter

1 cup shredded Cheddar cheese

1 teaspoon salt

¼ teaspoon black pepper

⅛ teaspoon cayenne pepper

1. Add all ingredients to a 4-quart slow cooker.
2. Cover and cook on low heat for 6–9 hours.

Almond and Dried Cherry Granola

5 cups old-fashioned rolled oats

1 cup slivered almonds

¼ cup agave nectar

¼ cup canola oil

1 teaspoon vanilla extract

½ cup dried tart cherries

¼ cup unsweetened flaked coconut

½ cup sunflower seeds

1. Place the oats and almonds into a 4-quart slow cooker. Drizzle with agave nectar, oil, and vanilla. Stir the mixture to distribute the syrup evenly.

2. Cook on high, uncovered, for 1½ hours, stirring every 15–20 minutes.

3. Add the cherries, coconut, and sunflower seeds.

4. Reduce heat to low. Cook for 4 hours, uncovered, stirring every 20 minutes.

5. Allow the granola to cool fully, and then store it in an airtight container for up to 1 month.

French Toast Casserole

12 slices whole-grain raisin bread

6 eggs

1 teaspoon vanilla extract

2 cups fat-free evaporated milk

2 tablespoons dark brown sugar

1 teaspoon cinnamon

¼ teaspoon nutmeg

1. Spray a 4-quart slow cooker with nonstick spray. Layer the bread in the slow cooker.
2. In a small bowl, whisk the eggs, vanilla, evaporated milk, brown sugar, cinnamon, and nutmeg.
3. Pour over the bread.
4. Cover and cook on low for 6–8 hours.
5. Remove the lid and cook uncovered for 30 minutes, or until the liquid has evaporated.

Onion, Pepper, and Potato Hash

2 tablespoons olive oil

4 cups peeled and grated russet potatoes

½ small onion, diced

1 poblano pepper, seeded and diced

2 cloves garlic, minced

1 teaspoon chili powder

½ teaspoon paprika

½ teaspoon cumin

1 teaspoon salt

¼ teaspoon black pepper

1. Add all ingredients to a 4-quart slow cooker.
2. Cover and cook on high heat for 4 hours.

Slow Cooker Suggestions

After you have grated the potatoes for the hash browns, make sure to rinse them in a colander to get rid of the extra starch. Then, allow the potatoes to dry so they will get extra crispy in the slow cooker.

Breakfast Casserole

¼ cup olive oil

3 cups peeled and grated potatoes

1 large onion, diced

½ green bell pepper, seeded and chopped

6 eggs, beaten

1 cup cottage cheese

2 cups Cheddar cheese

1 teaspoon salt

¼ teaspoon black pepper

1. Add all ingredients to a 4-quart slow cooker.
2. Cover and cook on low heat for 4 hours.

Spicy Breakfast Burrito

¼ cup olive oil

1 (16-ounce) package firm tofu, drained and crumbled

¼ cup diced red onion

1 tablespoon minced jalapeño

¼ cup diced red bell pepper

¼ cup diced poblano pepper

1 cup cooked black beans, drained

2 teaspoons turmeric

1 teaspoon cumin

½ teaspoon chili powder

1 teaspoon salt

¼ teaspoon black pepper

4 large flour tortillas

1 avocado, peeled and sliced

½ cup diced tomatoes

¼ cup chopped fresh cilantro

½ cup chipotle salsa

½ cup shredded Cheddar cheese

1. Add olive oil, tofu, onion, jalapeño, red bell pepper, and poblano pepper to a skillet and sauté on medium-high heat for 5–8 minutes. Place the mixture in a 4-quart slow cooker.

2. Add the black beans, turmeric, cumin, chili powder, salt, and black pepper. Cover and cook on low heat for 4 hours.

3. Scoop the filling onto the tortillas and add the avocado, tomato, cilantro, salsa, and cheese.

4. Fold the sides of the tortilla in and roll up the burrito.

Slow Cooker Suggestions

For best results, steam the tortillas on the stovetop using a steamer basket. If you're in a hurry, place the tortillas into the microwave one at a time and heat for about 30 seconds each.

Tofu Ranchero

3 tablespoons olive oil

1 (16-ounce) package firm tofu, drained and crumbled

1/2 medium onion, diced

2 cloves garlic, minced

1 lemon, juiced

1/2 teaspoon turmeric

1 teaspoon salt

1/4 teaspoon black pepper

1 cup cooked pinto beans, drained

8 corn tortillas

1/2 cup shredded Cheddar cheese

1/2 cup chipotle salsa

1. Add the olive oil, tofu, onion, garlic, lemon, turmeric, salt, black pepper, and pinto beans to a 4-quart slow cooker.
2. Cover and cook on low heat for 4 hours.
3. When the ranchero filling is nearly done, brown the tortillas on both sides using a small sauté pan.
4. Preheat the oven to 350°F.
5. Place the tortillas on a baking sheet and add the filling.
6. Sprinkle the cheese over the rancheros and bake until the cheese has melted, about 5 minutes. Top with the chipotle salsa.

Slow Cooker Suggestions

Salsa comes in many delicious and unique varieties. Most are clearly labeled mild, medium, and hot, but one's interpretation of those words can vary greatly. Chipotle salsa has a deep, earthy spice, but you can also use plain tomato salsa or tomatillo salsa in this recipe.

Rosemary Home Fries

¼ cup olive oil

4 cups diced red potatoes

½ small red onion, diced

1 poblano pepper, seeded and diced

½ red bell pepper, seeded and diced

1 teaspoon salt

¼ teaspoon black pepper

2 tablespoons chopped fresh rosemary

1. Add all ingredients, except for the rosemary, to a 4-quart slow cooker.
2. Cover and cook on low heat for 6 hours.
3. About 10 minutes before the potatoes are done, add the rosemary and cook for the remainder of the time.

Tempeh Sausage Scramble

1 (13-ounce) package tempeh, crumbled

1 (14-ounce) package extra-firm tofu, drained and crumbled

1 teaspoon dried sage

2 teaspoons brown sugar

⅛ teaspoon red pepper flakes

⅛ teaspoon dried marjoram

½ cup vegetarian "chicken" broth

1 teaspoon salt

¼ teaspoon black pepper

1. Add all ingredients to a 4-quart slow cooker.
2. Cover and cook on low heat for 4 hours.

Tempeh Bacon Bake

1 (13-ounce) package tempeh, cut into
   bite-sized pieces

2 tablespoons soy sauce

1 teaspoon liquid smoke

2 tablespoons apple cider vinegar

1 tablespoon brown sugar

2 pounds red potatoes, peeled and chopped

2 cups diced tomatoes

1 large onion, chopped

1 green bell pepper, seeded and chopped

1 teaspoon salt

¼ teaspoon black pepper

1. Place all ingredients in a 4-quart slow cooker.
2. Cover and cook on high 2 hours.

Jalapeño Hash Browns

2 tablespoons olive oil

2 pounds red potatoes, peeled and shredded

1 large onion, diced

¼ cup chopped pickled jalapeños

1 teaspoon salt

¼ teaspoon black pepper

1. Place all ingredients in a 4-quart slow cooker.
2. Cover and cook on high 2 hours.

CHAPTER 3

Appetizers and Snacks

Broccoli Dip

4 cups steamed broccoli florets

1 cup fresh baby spinach

1 shallot

1 jalapeño, seeded

1 tablespoon vegan Worcestershire sauce

½ tablespoon nonpareil capers

8 ounces cream cheese

8 ounces sour cream

¼ teaspoon black pepper

2 tablespoons lemon juice

1. Bring about 1" of water to boil in a large heavy-bottomed pot.
2. Add the vegetables and cook until fork-tender but not soft, about 3 minutes. Drain.
3. In a food processor, place the broccoli, spinach, shallot, jalapeño, Worcestershire sauce, and capers. Pulse until the mixture is mostly smooth.
4. Add the cream cheese, sour cream, pepper, and lemon juice.
5. Pulse until smooth.
6. Pour into a 1.5- or 2-quart slow cooker. Cover and cook on low for 1 hour.

Frijole Dip

2 (15-ounce) cans pinto beans, drained

1½ cups water

1 tablespoon olive oil

1 small onion, diced

3 cloves garlic, minced

1 cup diced tomato

1 teaspoon chipotle powder

½ teaspoon cumin

¼ cup finely chopped fresh cilantro

¼ teaspoon salt

1 cup grated Monterey jack cheese

1. In a 4-quart slow cooker, add the beans, water, olive oil, onion, and garlic.
2. Cover and cook over low heat for 1 hour.
3. Mash the beans until about ½ are smooth and ½ are still chunky.
4. Add all remaining ingredients; stir well and cook for an additional 30 minutes.

Sun-Dried Tomato Pesto Dip

SERVES
20

2 cloves garlic

1 tablespoon reduced-fat mayonnaise

1½ tablespoons minced fresh basil

1 teaspoon toasted pine nuts

¼ teaspoon white pepper

¼ cup dry (not oil-packed) sun-dried tomatoes, julienne cut

8 ounces reduced-fat cream cheese, room temperature

1. In a food processor, place the garlic, mayonnaise, basil, pine nuts, and pepper. Pulse until a fairly smooth paste forms.
2. Add the sun-dried tomatoes and pulse 4–5 times.
3. Add the cream cheese and pulse until smooth.
4. Scrape into a 2-quart slow cooker.
5. Cook on low for 1 hour. Stir before serving.

Slow Cooker Suggestions

To toast pine nuts, first preheat the oven to 350°F. Place the pine nuts on a cookie sheet or cake pan. Roast for 5–8 minutes in the oven. Pine nuts will be slightly browned and fragrant when fully toasted. Cool before using.

Spicy Seitan Buffalo Strips

⅓ cup Earth Balance Original Buttery Spread

⅓ cup hot sauce

1 tablespoon vinegar

1 teaspoon garlic powder

2 (7-ounce) packages Gardein Chick'n Strips

1. Place the Earth Balance in a small bowl and microwave for 30 seconds, or until melted.
2. Add the hot sauce, vinegar, and garlic powder, and stir well.
3. In a 4-quart slow cooker, add the prepared hot sauce mixture and Chick'n Strips, and cook over low heat for 1 hour.

Slow Cooker Suggestions

Faux buffalo chicken strips can be added to sandwiches or salads, but if you'd like to serve them as an appetizer or snack, place in a small basket lined with parchment paper and add a side of celery sticks, carrot sticks, and vegan ranch.

Baba Gannouj

2 tablespoons extra-virgin olive oil, divided

1 large eggplant, peeled and diced

4 cloves garlic, minced

½ cup water

3 tablespoons chopped fresh parsley

½ teaspoon salt

2 tablespoons fresh lemon juice

2 tablespoons tahini

1. In a 4-quart slow cooker, add 1 tablespoon olive oil, eggplant, garlic, and water, and stir until coated.
2. Cover and cook on high heat for 4 hours.
3. Strain the cooked eggplant and garlic and add to a food processor or blender along with the parsley, salt, lemon juice, and tahini. Pulse to process.
4. Scrape down the side of the food processor or blender container with a spatula if necessary.
5. Add the remaining olive oil and process until smooth.

Zesty Lemon Hummus

1 pound dried chickpeas

Water, as needed

3 tablespoons tahini

4 tablespoons lemon juice

Zest of 1 lemon

3 cloves garlic

¼ teaspoon salt

1. In a 4-quart slow cooker, place the chickpeas and cover with water.
2. Soak overnight. The next day, drain and rinse the chickpeas and return them to the slow cooker.
3. Cover them with water and cook on low for 8 hours. Drain, reserving the liquid.
4. In a food processor, place the chickpeas, tahini, lemon juice, lemon zest, garlic, and salt.
5. Pulse until smooth, adding the reserved liquid as needed to achieve the desired texture.

Slow Cooker Suggestions

Keeping hummus and fresh vegetables around makes healthy snacking easy. Just cut carrots, celery, and radishes into snack-friendly sizes, and place them in a bowl with a tight fitting lid. Fill the bowl ⅔ with water. They will stay crisp in the refrigerator for up to one week.

Marinated Mushrooms and Garlic

2 (8-ounce) packages
   mushrooms

5 cloves garlic, minced

1 cup red wine

1 cup soy sauce

1 cup water

½ teaspoon dried tarragon

⅛ teaspoon salt

⅛ teaspoon black
   pepper

Add all ingredients to a 4-quart slow cooker, cover, and cook on high heat for 3–4 hours.

Kalamata Olive Hummus

1 pound dry chickpeas

7 cups water

⅓ cup tahini

2 lemons, juiced

¼ cup chopped kalamata olives

2 cloves garlic, minced

4 tablespoons olive oil

2 teaspoons cumin

¾ teaspoon salt

¼ teaspoon black pepper

1. Place the dry chickpeas and water in a 4-quart slow cooker, cover, and cook on high heat for 4 hours.
2. Drain the chickpeas.
3. Combine the chickpeas and the rest of the ingredients in a food processor and purée until smooth.

Slow Cooker Suggestions

Hummus is a great source of protein and iron, making it an excellent choice for vegans. Even kids love the creamy treat!

Spinach and Artichoke Dip

SERVES 6

2 tablespoons Earth Balance Original Buttery Spread

½ medium onion, diced

1 clove garlic, minced

2 teaspoons flour

2 cups unsweetened almond milk

1 lemon, juiced

1 (1-pound) bag frozen spinach, thawed, with water squeezed out

1 (14-ounce) can artichokes, drained and chopped

⅛ teaspoon nutmeg

⅛ teaspoon salt

⅛ teaspoon black pepper

1. Add the Earth Balance to a sauté pan, and sauté the onion and garlic on medium-high heat for 3–4 minutes.
2. Stir in the flour until the mixture is smooth, then place the mixture in a 4-quart slow cooker.
3. Add the remaining ingredients, stir, cover, and cook on high heat for 2–3 hours.

Edamame-Miso Dip

SERVES 4

½ pound frozen shelled edamame

3 cups water

1 tablespoon soy sauce

2½ tablespoons miso paste

2 green onions, thinly sliced

⅛ teaspoon salt

1. Add all ingredients to a 4-quart slow cooker, stir, cover, and cook on low heat for 2 hours, or until the edamame is tender.
2. Using a slotted spoon, remove the edamame and place it in a food processor or blender.
3. Purée the edamame, adding enough of the cooking liquid to create a smooth consistency. Serve cold or at room temperature.

Parsley and Thyme White Bean Dip

SERVES 6

2 tablespoons olive oil

½ medium onion, diced

3 cloves garlic, minced

½ pound dry white beans

3 cups water

1 lemon, juiced

1 tablespoon chopped fresh parsley

½ tablespoon minced fresh thyme

¼ teaspoon salt

⅛ teaspoon black pepper

1. Add the olive oil to a sauté pan and sauté the onion and garlic on medium-high heat for 3–4 minutes, then place the mixture in a 4-quart slow cooker.
2. Add the dry white beans and water to the slow cooker.
3. Cover and cook on high heat for 4–5 hours, or until the beans are tender. Drain the white beans, reserving some water.
4. In a food processor, purée the white beans, adding enough water to create a smooth consistency.
5. Add the lemon juice, parsley, thyme, salt, and pepper, and continue to blend until very smooth.
6. Cover and refrigerate for at least 2 hours before serving.

Slow Cooker Suggestions

Don't substitute fresh herbs with the dried variety in this recipe. Fresh herbs are needed to complement the lemon and give the dip a light and refreshing flavor.

Pintos, Cerveza, and Lime Dip

SERVES
6

2 tablespoons olive oil

½ small onion, diced

3 cloves garlic, minced

½ pound dry pinto beans

3 cups water

1 (12-ounce) bottle Mexican beer

1 jalapeño, seeded and minced

2 limes, juiced

¼ teaspoon salt

⅛ teaspoon black pepper

1. Add the olive oil to the sauté pan and sauté the onion and garlic on medium-high heat for 3–4 minutes.
2. Place the mixture in a 4-quart slow cooker.
3. Add the dry pinto beans, water, and beer to the slow cooker.
4. Cover and cook on high heat for 4–5 hours, or until the beans are tender. Drain the pinto beans, reserving some water.
5. In a food processor, purée the pinto beans, minced jalapeño, lime juice, salt, and pepper, adding enough water to create a smooth consistency. Serve hot or at room temperature.

Garlic Confit

3 cups olive oil

5 heads of garlic, with cloves peeled

3 dried red chilies

1. Add all ingredients to a 4-quart slow cooker. Make sure there is enough oil to cover all the garlic cloves.
2. Place the cover on the slow cooker and cook on low heat for 4 hours, or until the garlic is tender.
3. Remove the garlic with a slotted spoon and place in canning jars. Pour the oil over the garlic and seal the top.

Slow Cooker Suggestions

Garlic confit is a great and easy way to preserve garlic when it is in season and at its peak. Garlic prepared using this method can be jarred and stored for up to 3 months.

Orange-Pomegranate Tempeh Bites

1 (13-ounce) package tempeh, cut into bite-sized squares

1 tablespoon olive oil

¼ cup soy sauce

¼ cup teriyaki glaze

2 tablespoons brown sugar

3 oranges, juiced

¼ cup pomegranate juice

1. Add all ingredients to a 4-quart slow cooker.
2. Cover and cook on high heat for 2 hours.

CHAPTER 4

Soups, Stews, and Chilis

Vegetable Broth

2 large onions, halved

2 medium carrots, cut into large pieces

3 stalks celery, cut in half

1 whole head garlic, crushed

10 whole peppercorns

1 bay leaf

6 cups water

1. Add all ingredients to a 4-quart slow cooker.
2. Cover and cook on low heat for 8–10 hours.
3. Strain the broth to remove the vegetables, herbs, and spices. Store in the refrigerator.

Slow Cooker Suggestions

Homemade broth can be stored in a covered container in the refrigerator for 2–3 days, or frozen for up to 3 months.

No-Beef Broth

4 medium carrots, cut into large pieces

2 large onions, quartered

1 stalk celery, chopped

2 cups fresh portobello mushrooms, sliced

1 whole head garlic, crushed

1 tablespoon vegan Worcestershire sauce

1 tablespoon brown sugar

6 cups water

1. In a 4-quart slow cooker, add all ingredients.
2. Cover and cook on low heat for 8–10 hours.
3. Strain the broth to remove the vegetables. Store the broth in a covered container in the refrigerator for 2–3 days, or frozen for up to 3 months.

Beer-Cheese Soup

½ cup butter or vegan margarine

½ medium white onion, diced

2 medium carrots, diced

2 stalks celery, diced

½ cup flour

3 cups Vegetable Broth (see recipe in this chapter)

1 (12-ounce) bottle pale ale beer

3 cups milk or unsweetened soymilk

3 cups Cheddar cheese

1 teaspoon salt

1 teaspoon black pepper

½ teaspoon ground mustard

1. In a sauté pan over medium heat, melt the butter or vegan margarine, then sauté the onion, carrots, and celery until just softened, 5–7 minutes.
2. Add the flour and stir to form a roux. Let cook for 2–3 minutes.
3. In a 4-quart slow cooker, add the cooked vegetables and roux, then slowly pour in the broth and beer while whisking.
4. Add the milk, cheese, salt, pepper, and mustard.
5. Cover and cook on low for 4 hours.
6. Let the soup cool slightly, then blend until smooth, or you can skip this step and serve chunky.

Slow Cooker Suggestions

Plain or original soymilk typically contains sugar and has a distinct flavor that will stand out in savory dishes. For these recipes, use plain unsweetened soymilk instead.

Tomato Basil Soup

2 tablespoons Earth Balance Original Buttery Spread

½ small onion, diced

2 cloves garlic, minced

1 (28-ounce) can whole peeled tomatoes

½ cup Vegetable Broth (see recipe in this chapter)

1 bay leaf

1 teaspoon salt

1 teaspoon black pepper

½ cup unsweetened soymilk

¼ cup sliced fresh basil

1. In a sauté pan over medium heat, melt the Earth Balance, then sauté the onion and garlic for 3–4 minutes.
2. In a 4-quart slow cooker, add the onion and garlic, tomatoes, Vegetable Broth, bay leaf, salt, and pepper.
3. Cover and cook over low heat 4 hours.
4. Allow to cool slightly, then remove the bay leaf. Process the soup in a blender or immersion blender.
5. Return the soup to the slow cooker, then add the soymilk and basil; heat on low for an additional 30 minutes.

Minestrone Soup

3 cloves garlic, minced

1 (15-ounce) can fire-roasted diced tomatoes

1 (28-ounce) can crushed tomatoes

2 stalks celery, diced

1 medium onion, diced

3 medium carrots, diced

3 cups Vegetable Broth (see recipe in this chapter)

2 (15-ounce) cans kidney beans, drained and rinsed

2 tablespoons tomato paste

2 tablespoons minced fresh basil

2 tablespoons minced fresh oregano

2 tablespoons minced fresh Italian parsley

1½ cups shredded cabbage

¾ cup diced zucchini

1 teaspoon salt

½ teaspoon black pepper

8 ounces small cooked pasta

1. In a 4-quart slow cooker, add the garlic, diced and crushed tomatoes, celery, onions, carrots, Vegetable Broth, beans, tomato paste, basil, oregano, and parsley.
2. Cover and cook on low heat for 6–8 hours.
3. Add shredded cabbage and zucchini, and turn to high for the last hour.
4. Stir in the salt, pepper, and pasta before serving.

Slow Cooker Suggestions

Anchellini, small shells, hoops, alfabeto, or ditaletti are all small pasta shapes suitable for soup. For heartier soups, try bow ties or rotini. Thin rice noodles or vermicelli are better for Asian-style soups.

French Onion Soup

¼ cup olive oil

4 large Vidalia onions, sliced

4 cloves garlic, minced

1 tablespoon dried thyme

1 cup red wine

4 cups Vegetable Broth (see recipe in this chapter)

1 teaspoon salt

1 teaspoon black pepper

4 slices French bread

4 ounces shredded mozzarella cheese

1. In a sauté pan, heat the olive oil over medium-high heat and cook the onions until golden brown, about 3 minutes.

2. Add the garlic and sauté for 1 minute.

3. In a 4-quart slow cooker, pour the sautéed vegetables, thyme, red wine, Vegetable Broth, salt, and pepper.

4. Cover and cook on low heat for 4 hours.

5. While the soup is cooking, preheat the oven to the broiler setting. Lightly toast the slices of French bread.

6. To serve, ladle the soup into a broiler-safe bowl, place a slice of the toasted French bread on top of the soup, sprinkle the cheese on top of the bread, and place the soup under the broiler until the cheese has melted.

Roasted Red Pepper and Corn Soup

6 red bell peppers, halved and seeded

1 cup corn kernels

1 large russet potato, peeled and chopped

½ medium white onion, diced

2 cloves garlic, minced

6 cups Vegetable Broth (see recipe in this chapter)

2 tablespoons white wine vinegar

2 bay leaves

¼ teaspoon black pepper

1 teaspoon salt

2 tablespoons chopped fresh cilantro

1. Preheat your oven's broiler.
2. Place the bell peppers on a baking sheet, skin-side up, and broil for 15 minutes or until black spots appear.
3. Remove and place the peppers in a paper or plastic bag. Close the bag and let sit for 5 minutes to loosen the skins. Remove the peppers, peel off the skin, and chop.
4. Place the peppers and all remaining ingredients, except cilantro, in a 6-quart slow cooker.
5. Cover and cook over low heat for 6 hours. Remove bay leaves when done.
6. Purée using an immersion blender or traditional blender. Add the cilantro before serving.

Vegetable Dumpling Stew

2 tablespoons olive oil

½ large onion, diced

2 cloves garlic, minced

2 large carrots, chopped

2 stalks celery, chopped

½ cup corn kernels

½ cup okra, chopped

2 (14.5-ounce) cans diced tomatoes

4 cups Vegetable Broth (see recipe in this chapter)

¼ teaspoon dried rosemary

1 teaspoon dried parsley

¼ teaspoon dried oregano

½ teaspoon salt

¼ teaspoon black pepper

1 (6-ounce) package refrigerated biscuits

Flour, for dusting

1. In a sauté pan over medium heat, add the olive oil, onion, and garlic and sauté for 3 minutes.
2. In a 4-quart slow cooker, add all ingredients except for the biscuits and flour.
3. Cover and cook on low heat for 4–5 hours.
4. While the stew is cooking, flatten the biscuits with a rolling pin on a floured surface, then cut each into fourths.
5. Drop the biscuit pieces into the stew and cook for 30 more minutes.

Super Greens Stew

2 cups chopped kale

2 cups chopped Swiss chard

1 (15-ounce) can chickpeas, drained

¼ large onion, diced

1 large carrot, sliced

2 cloves garlic, minced

6 cups Vegetable Broth (see recipe in this chapter)

1½ teaspoons salt

½ teaspoon black pepper

1 sprig rosemary

½ teaspoon dried marjoram

1. In a 4-quart slow cooker, add all ingredients.
2. Cover and cook on low heat for 6 hours.

Wild Mushroom Ragout

2 tablespoons olive oil

1 large onion, diced

½ pound white button mushrooms, sliced

½ pound shiitake mushrooms, sliced

½ pound oyster mushrooms, sliced

3 cloves garlic, minced

¼ teaspoon salt

⅛ teaspoon black pepper

1 tablespoon chopped fresh rosemary

1 tablespoon chopped fresh sage

2 cups diced tomatoes

2 cups Vegetable Broth (see recipe in this chapter)

1. Add the olive oil to a sauté pan and sauté the onion and all mushrooms on medium-high heat for 4–5 minutes.
2. Add the garlic, salt, and black pepper and sauté for 1 minute more then add to a 4-quart slow cooker.
3. Add the rosemary, sage, tomatoes, and Vegetable Broth and cook on low heat for 2 hours.

Slow Cooker Suggestions

Button mushrooms are a milder type of mushroom with little flavor, but they are inexpensive and can be used in combination with more flavorful varieties. Shiitake, oyster, chanterelle, and hen of the woods are more expensive varieties that have wonderful texture and flavor.

New England Corn Chowder

½ cup Earth Balance Original Buttery Spread

1 medium onion, diced

3 cloves garlic, minced

¼ cup flour

4 cups unsweetened soymilk

3 large potatoes, peeled and diced

2 cups frozen corn

2 cups Vegetable Broth (see recipe in this chapter)

½ teaspoon dried thyme

½ teaspoon salt

1. Add the Earth Balance to a sauté pan and sauté the onion on medium heat for 4–5 minutes.
2. Add the garlic and sauté for 1 minute more.
3. Slowly stir in the flour with a whisk and create a roux. Stir in the soymilk and continue whisking until very smooth.
4. In a 4-quart slow cooker, add the cooked vegetables and roux, then add the remaining ingredients and cook on low heat for 3–4 hours.

Southwest Vegetable Chili

1 (28-ounce) can diced tomatoes

1 (15-ounce) can red kidney beans

1 medium onion, chopped

1 green bell pepper, seeded and chopped

1 red bell pepper, seeded and chopped

1 medium zucchini, chopped

1 squash, chopped

¼ cup chopped pickled jalapeños

2 tablespoons chili powder

2 tablespoons garlic powder

2 tablespoons cumin

1 teaspoon chipotle powder

⅛ teaspoon dried thyme

¼ teaspoon black pepper

1. Add all ingredients to a 4-quart slow cooker.
2. Cover and cook on low heat for 5 hours.

Five-Pepper Chili

SERVES 8

1 medium onion, diced

1 jalapeño, seeded and minced

1 habanero pepper, seeded and minced

1 bell pepper, seeded and diced

1 poblano pepper, seeded and diced

2 cloves garlic, minced

2 (15-ounce) cans crushed tomatoes

2 cups diced fresh tomatoes

2 tablespoons chili powder

1 tablespoon cumin

1½ teaspoons cayenne pepper

2 tablespoons vegan Worcestershire sauce

2 (15-ounce) cans pinto beans

1 teaspoon salt

¼ teaspoon black pepper

1. Add all ingredients to a 4-quart slow cooker.
2. Cover and cook on low heat for 5 hours.

Slow Cooker Suggestions

Since peppers vary greatly in regard to how hot they are, the Scoville scale was designed to measure this heat. Here are the peppers in this recipe, from mildest to hottest: bell, poblano, jalapeño, and habanero.

Black Bean, Corn, and Fresh Tomato Chili

1 medium red onion, diced

1 jalapeño, seeded and minced

3 cloves garlic, minced

1 (15-ounce) can black beans, drained

1 (15-ounce) can corn, drained

3 tablespoons chili powder

1 tablespoon paprika

1 teaspoon dried oregano

1 teaspoon cumin

½ teaspoon chipotle powder

2 cups Vegetable Broth (see recipe in this chapter)

½ teaspoon salt

¼ teaspoon black pepper

2 cups diced tomatoes

¼ cup chopped fresh cilantro

4 tablespoons sour cream

1. In a 4-quart slow cooker, add all ingredients except tomatoes, cilantro, and sour cream.
2. Cover and cook on low heat for 5 hours.
3. When the chili is done cooking, mix in the tomatoes and garnish with the cilantro.
4. Top with sour cream.

CHAPTER 5

Vegetables and Beans

Gingered Sweet Potatoes

2½ pounds sweet potatoes

1 cup water

1 tablespoon grated fresh ginger

½ tablespoon minced uncrystallized candied ginger

½ tablespoon butter

1. Peel and quarter the sweet potatoes. Add them to a 4-quart slow cooker.
2. Add the water, fresh ginger, and candied ginger. Stir.
3. Cook on high for 3–4 hours, or until the potatoes are tender.
4. Add the butter and mash. Serve immediately, or turn them down to low to keep warm for up to 3 hours.

Cranberry-Walnut Brussels Sprouts

1 pound Brussels sprouts, trimmed and quartered

2 tablespoons olive oil

2 tablespoons water

½ teaspoon salt

¼ teaspoon black pepper

¼ cup dried cranberries

¼ cup chopped walnuts

1. Place all ingredients in a 2-quart slow cooker.
2. Stir until the olive oil coats the other ingredients.
3. Cover and cook on high heat for 2½ hours.

Baby Bok Choy

2 tablespoons soy sauce

2 tablespoons apple cider vinegar

2 tablespoons sesame oil

½ teaspoon garlic powder

1 teaspoon red pepper flakes

3 heads baby bok choy, halved lengthwise

1. In a small bowl, whisk together all ingredients except for the bok choy.
2. Place the bok choy in a 4-quart slow cooker; pour the soy sauce mixture over the bok choy.
3. Cover and cook on low heat for 3 hours.

Creamed Spinach

1 tablespoon butter

1 clove garlic, minced

1 tablespoon flour

1 cup unsweetened soymilk

½ teaspoon salt

½ teaspoon red pepper flakes

¼ teaspoon dried sage

1 (12-ounce) package frozen spinach, thawed

1. Melt the butter in a 2-quart slow cooker on high heat.
2. Add the garlic and cook for 2 minutes, then stir in the flour.
3. Slowly pour in the soymilk and whisk until all lumps are removed.
4. Add all remaining ingredients. Stir and cook on low heat for 2 hours.

Stuffed Peppers

4 large bell peppers

½ teaspoon chipotle powder

¼ teaspoon hot Mexican chili powder

¼ teaspoon black pepper

⅛ teaspoon salt

1 (15-ounce) can fire-roasted diced tomatoes with garlic

1 cup cooked long-grain rice

1½ cups broccoli florets

¼ cup diced onion

½ cup water

1. Cut the tops off of each pepper to form a cap. Remove the seeds from the cap. Remove the seeds and most of the ribs from inside the pepper.
2. Place the peppers open-side up in a 4- or 6-quart slow cooker.
3. In a medium bowl, mix the spices, tomatoes, rice, broccoli, and onions.
4. Spoon the mixture into each pepper until they are filled to the top. Replace the cap.
5. Pour the water into the bottom of the slow cooker insert.
6. Cook on low for 6 hours.

Eggplant "Lasagna"

2 (1-pound) eggplants

2 teaspoons olive oil, divided

1 medium onion, diced

3 cloves garlic, minced

1 tablespoon minced fresh Italian parsley

1 tablespoon minced fresh basil

1 (28-ounce) can crushed tomatoes

1 shallot, diced

4 ounces fresh spinach

1 tablespoon dried mixed Italian seasoning

1/4 teaspoon salt

1/2 teaspoon black pepper

30 ounces ricotta cheese

1. Slice the eggplants lengthwise into 1/4"-thick slices. Set aside.

2. Heat 1 teaspoon olive oil in a nonstick pan over medium heat. Sauté the onion and garlic until just softened, 1–2 minutes.

3. Add the parsley, basil, and crushed tomatoes. Sauté until the sauce thickens and the liquid has evaporated, about 20 minutes.

4. In a second nonstick pan, heat the remaining oil over medium heat. Sauté the shallot and spinach until the spinach has wilted, about 30 seconds to 1 minute. Drain off any extra liquid.

5. Stir the shallot-spinach mixture, Italian seasoning, salt, and pepper into the ricotta. Set aside.

6. Preheat the oven to 375°F. Place the eggplant slices on baking sheets. Bake for 10 minutes. Cool slightly.

7. Pour 1/3 of the sauce onto the bottom of a 4-quart slow cooker. Top with a single layer of eggplant. Top with 1/2 of the cheese mixture. Add 1/3 of the sauce. Top with the rest of the cheese mixture. Layer the remaining eggplant on top, then top with remaining sauce.

8. Cover and cook for 4 hours on low, then cook uncovered for 30 minutes on high.

Eggplant Caponata

2 (1-pound) eggplants

1 teaspoon olive oil

1 medium red onion, diced

4 cloves garlic, minced

1 stalk celery, diced

2 tomatoes, diced

2 tablespoons nonpareil capers

2 tablespoons toasted pine nuts

1 teaspoon red pepper flakes

¼ cup red wine vinegar

1. Pierce the eggplants with a fork. Cook on high in a 4- or 6-quart slow cooker for 2 hours.
2. Allow to cool. Peel off the skin. Slice each in half and remove the seeds. Discard the skin and seeds.
3. Place the pulp in a food processor. Pulse until smooth. Set aside.
4. Heat the oil in a nonstick skillet. Sauté the onion, garlic, and celery until the onion is soft, about 5 minutes.
5. Add the eggplant and tomatoes. Sauté 3 minutes.
6. Return to the slow cooker and add the capers, pine nuts, red pepper flakes, and vinegar. Stir.
7. Cook on low for 30 minutes. Stir prior to serving.

Caramelized Onions

4 pounds Vidalia onions

3 tablespoons Earth Balance Original Buttery Spread

1 tablespoon balsamic vinegar

1. Peel and slice the onions into ¼" slices. Separate them into rings.
2. Place the onions into a 4-quart slow cooker.
3. Scatter chunks of the Earth Balance over the top of the onions and drizzle with balsamic vinegar.
4. Cover and cook on low for 10 hours.
5. If after 10 hours the onions are wet, turn the slow cooker up to high and cook uncovered for an additional 30 minutes, or until the liquid evaporates.

Slow Cooker Suggestions

Store the onions in an airtight container. They will keep for up to 2 weeks refrigerated or up to 6 months frozen. If frozen, defrost overnight in the refrigerator before using.

Zucchini Ragout

5 ounces fresh spinach

3 medium zucchini, diced

½ cup diced red onion

2 stalks celery, diced

2 medium carrots, diced

1 parsnip, diced

3 tablespoons tomato paste

¼ cup water

1 teaspoon black pepper

¼ teaspoon kosher salt

1 tablespoon minced fresh basil

1 tablespoon minced fresh Italian parsley

1 tablespoon minced fresh oregano

1. Place all ingredients into a 4-quart slow cooker. Stir.
2. Cook on low for 4 hours. Stir before serving.

Slow Cooker Suggestions

The cost of herbs can add up quickly, but you can save a little money by shopping at a farmers' market or buying a blend of spices (an Italian blend would work well in this recipe) instead of buying each individually.

Meatless Moussaka

SERVES
8

¾ cup dry brown or yellow lentils, rinsed and drained

2 large potatoes, peeled and diced

1 cup water

1 stalk celery, finely diced

1 medium sweet onion, diced

3 cloves garlic, minced

½ teaspoon salt

¼ teaspoon cinnamon

¼ teaspoon freshly grated nutmeg

¼ teaspoon black pepper

¼ teaspoon dried basil

¼ teaspoon dried oregano

¼ teaspoon dried parsley

1 medium eggplant, diced

12 baby carrots, each cut into 3 pieces

2 cups diced Roma tomatoes

1 (8-ounce) package cream cheese, softened

1. Add the lentils, potatoes, water, celery, onion, garlic, salt, cinnamon, nutmeg, pepper, basil, oregano, and parsley to a 4-quart slow cooker. Stir.
2. Top with eggplant and carrots.
3. Cover and cook on low for 6 hours, or until the lentils are cooked through.
4. Stir in the tomatoes and cream cheese over lentil mixture. Cover and cook on low for an additional 30 minutes.

Slow Cooker Suggestions

Moussaka is traditionally made with minced meat, but you can easily vegetarianize this classic Greek and Arabic dish by using an abundance of vegetables instead. It can be served either warm or cold.

Rosemary-Thyme Green Beans

1 pound green beans

1 tablespoon minced fresh rosemary

1 teaspoon minced fresh thyme

2 tablespoons lemon juice

2 tablespoons water

1. Place all ingredients into a 2-quart slow cooker. Stir to distribute the spices evenly.

2. Cook on low for 1½ hours, or until the green beans are tender. Stir before serving.

Herb-Stuffed Tomatoes

4 large tomatoes

1 cup cooked quinoa

1 stalk celery, minced

1 tablespoon minced fresh garlic

2 tablespoons minced fresh oregano

2 tablespoons minced fresh Italian parsley

1 teaspoon dried chervil

1 teaspoon fennel seeds

¾ cup water

1. Cut out the core of each tomato and discard. Scoop out the seeds, leaving the walls of the tomato intact.

2. In a small bowl, stir together the quinoa, celery, garlic, and spices. Divide evenly among the 4 tomatoes.

3. Place the filled tomatoes in a single layer in an oval 4-quart slow cooker.

4. Pour the water into the bottom of the slow cooker.

5. Cook on low for 4 hours.

Summary Squash Casserole

2 tablespoons Earth Balance Original Buttery Spread

½ medium white onion, diced

2 cloves garlic, minced

2 teaspoons cornstarch

2 tablespoons water

4 cups diced yellow squash

½ cup diced button mushrooms

1 cup unsweetened soymilk

¼ cup nutritional yeast

½ teaspoon salt

¼ teaspoon black pepper

30 Ritz Crackers, crushed

1. Melt the Earth Balance in a sauté pan over medium-high heat. Add the onion and sauté for 3 minutes.
2. Add the garlic and sauté for an additional minute. Add the onion and garlic mixture to a 4-quart slow cooker and turn the heat onto low.
3. Combine the cornstarch and water in a small bowl and whisk until all lumps have been removed.
4. Add cornstarch mixture, squash, mushrooms, soymilk, nutritional yeast, salt, pepper, and half of the crackers to the slow cooker, and stir until well combined.
5. Top with the remaining crackers.
6. Cover and cook on low heat for 4 hours.

Lime-Soaked Poblanos

SERVES 4

¼ cup lime juice

¼ cup water

2 cloves garlic, minced

2 tablespoons chopped fresh cilantro

½ teaspoon salt

4 poblano peppers, seeded and sliced

1. Combine all of the ingredients in a 4-quart slow cooker and stir until well combined.
2. Cover and cook on low heat for 4 hours.

Chipotle Corn on the Cob

SERVES 6

6 ears corn, shucked

Water, as needed

3 tablespoons Earth Balance Original Buttery Spread

½ teaspoon chipotle powder

½ teaspoon salt

1. Place the corn in a 4-quart slow cooker and cover with water until it is 1" from the top of the slow cooker.
2. Cook on high heat for 2 hours.
3. While the corn is cooking, combine the Earth Balance, chipotle powder, and salt in a small bowl.
4. When the corn is done cooking, rub a small spoonful of the Earth Balance mixture on each cob and then serve.

Curried Lentils

2 teaspoons canola oil

1 large onion, thinly sliced

2 cloves garlic, minced

2 jalapeños, seeded and diced

½ teaspoon red pepper flakes

½ teaspoon cumin

1 pound yellow lentils

6 cups water

½ teaspoon salt

½ teaspoon turmeric

4 cups chopped fresh spinach

1. Heat the oil in a nonstick pan over medium heat. Sauté the onion slices until they start to brown, 8–10 minutes.
2. Add the garlic, jalapeños, red pepper flakes, and cumin. Sauté for 2–3 minutes. Add the onion mixture to a 4-quart slow cooker.
3. Sort through the lentils and discard any rocks or foreign matter.
4. Add the lentils to the slow cooker. Stir in the water, salt, and turmeric.
5. Cover and cook on high for 2½ hours.
6. Add the spinach and stir. Cook on high for an additional 15 minutes.

Bourbon Baked Beans

1 large sweet onion, diced

3 (15-ounce) cans cannellini, great northern, or navy beans

1 (15-ounce) can diced tomatoes

¼ cup maple syrup

3 tablespoons apple cider vinegar

1 teaspoon liquid smoke

4 cloves garlic, minced

2 tablespoons ground mustard

1½ teaspoons black pepper

½ teaspoon ground ginger

¼ teaspoon red pepper flakes

2 tablespoons bourbon

1. Add all ingredients to a 4-quart slow cooker. Stir until combined.
2. Cover and cook on low heat for 6 hours.

Garlic and Sage Borlotti Beans

1 (16-ounce) bag dried borlotti beans

Water, enough to cover beans by 1"

2 teaspoons salt

2 tablespoons extra-virgin olive oil

4 cloves garlic, minced

2 cups diced tomatoes

1 teaspoon dried sage

¼ teaspoon black pepper

1. Add all of the ingredients to a 4-quart slow cooker.
2. Cover and cook on low heat for 6 hours. Check the beans at about 5 hours to see if they are tender and continue cooking if necessary. Serve as a side dish.

Slow Cooker Suggestions

Borlotti beans are commonly used in Italian and Greek cuisine and can be identified by their white skin and red speckles. They have a thick, meaty flavor and hold up well to heavy seasonings like garlic and dried sage. If you can't find them in your local supermarket, cannellini beans make an acceptable substitute.

Lentils with Sautéed Spinach, White Wine, and Garlic

1 (16-ounce) bag dried lentils

Water, enough to cover lentils by 1"

2 teaspoons salt, divided

2 tablespoons olive oil

8 cups fresh spinach

5 cloves garlic, minced

⅛ cup white wine

1 teaspoon black pepper

1. Add lentils, water, and 1 teaspoon of the salt to a 4-quart slow cooker.
2. Cover and cook on high heat for 3–4 hours. Check the lentils at about 3 hours, and continue cooking if necessary.
3. Once the lentils are done, drain in a colander and allow them to cool to room temperature.
4. While the lentils are cooling, add the olive oil to a large pan and sauté the spinach with the garlic and white wine over medium-low heat for 3–5 minutes.
5. In a large bowl, combine the lentils with the sautéed spinach and the remaining salt and pepper.

Slow Cooker Suggestions

As a general rule, if you wouldn't drink the wine, then don't cook with it. Also remember to consider how the flavor of the wine will pair with other ingredients. If you are trying to achieve a rich, earthy sauce, then don't use a floral or fruity white. Instead, choose an oaky Chardonnay.

Creole Red Beans

1 (16-ounce) bag dried red kidney beans

Water, enough to cover beans by 1"

2 teaspoons salt

1 tablespoon Cajun seasoning

2 teaspoons liquid smoke

1 teaspoon vegan Worcestershire sauce

2 teaspoons hot sauce

1 teaspoon dried thyme

2 teaspoons cayenne pepper

4 bay leaves

1. Add all ingredients to a 4-quart slow cooker.
2. Cover and cook on low heat for 6 hours.
3. Check the beans at about 5 hours to see if they are tender and continue cooking if necessary.

Slow Cooker Suggestions

Liquid smoke, which is found in the condiment aisle of grocery stores, is an easy way to add a smoky, hearty flavor to any dish. The concentrated liquid is made by condensing smoke (usually from burning hickory wood) to a liquid, or by channeling water through the smoke to pick up the smoky flavor. Some producers add additional flavoring such as vinegar and molasses.

Drunken Refried Beans

1 (16-ounce) bag dried pinto beans

Water, enough to cover beans by 1"

2 (12-ounce) bottles light-colored beer

2 teaspoons salt, divided

4 cloves garlic, minced

1. Add pinto beans, water, beer, and 1 teaspoon salt to a 4-quart slow cooker.
2. Cover and cook on low heat for 6 hours. Check the beans at about 5 hours to see if they are tender and continue cooking if necessary.
3. Once the beans are done, drain in a colander, reserving about 1 cup of the cooking liquid.
4. In a large bowl, combine the beans, remaining salt, and garlic.
5. Mash the bean mixture with a potato masher, adding the reserved cooking liquid as needed until a smooth consistency is reached.

CHAPTER 6

Potatoes, Rice, and Grains

Potato Risotto

2 leeks (white part only)

¼ cup olive oil

3 sprigs fresh thyme, chopped

3 pounds russet potatoes, peeled and finely diced

2 cups dry white wine

5 cups Vegetable Broth (see recipe in Chapter 4)

1 teaspoon salt

¼ teaspoon black pepper

4 cups fresh spinach

1. Thinly slice the leeks crosswise into semicircles and rinse.
2. Add the olive oil to a sauté pan and sauté the leeks on medium-high heat until translucent, 5–7 minutes.
3. Add leeks to a 4-quart slow cooker.
4. Add the rest of the ingredients except for the spinach.
5. Cover and cook on high heat for 4 hours.
6. Mix the spinach into the risotto and continue cooking for 1 more hour.

Potatoes Au Gratin

½ cup water

8 cups peeled and diced potatoes

2 cups Alfredo sauce

1 cup shredded Cheddar cheese

1 teaspoon salt

¼ teaspoon black pepper

1. Add all ingredients to a 4-quart slow cooker.
2. Cover and cook on high heat for 4 hours.

Chipotle and Thyme Sweet Potatoes

SERVES 6

6 cups cubed sweet potatoes

4 tablespoons butter

3 cloves garlic, minced

1 teaspoon chipotle powder

½ teaspoon dried thyme

1 teaspoon salt

¼ teaspoon black pepper

1. Add all ingredients to a 4-quart slow cooker.
2. Cover and cook on high heat for 4 hours.

Garlic-Parsley Potatoes

SERVES 8

½ cup butter or vegan margarine

6 cloves garlic, minced

1 large onion, diced

1½ pounds red potatoes, quartered

½ cup unsweetened soymilk

1 teaspoon salt

¼ teaspoon black pepper

¼ cup chopped fresh parsley

1 tablespoon fresh lemon juice

1. Add the butter or vegan margarine to a sauté pan and sauté the garlic and onions on high heat until they are golden brown, about 2–3 minutes. Add the garlic and onions to a 4-quart slow cooker.
2. Add the rest of the ingredients except for the parsley and lemon juice.
3. Cover and cook on high heat for 4 hours.
4. Mix in the parsley and lemon and cook for an additional 30 minutes.

Potatoes Paprikash

1½ teaspoons olive oil

1 medium onion, halved and sliced

1 shallot, minced

4 cloves garlic, minced

½ teaspoon salt

½ teaspoon caraway seeds

¼ teaspoon black pepper

1 teaspoon cayenne pepper

3 tablespoons paprika

2 pounds red skin potatoes, thinly sliced

2 cups Vegetable Broth (see recipe in Chapter 4)

2 tablespoons tomato paste

½ cup sour cream

1. In a small nonstick pan, heat the oil over medium heat.
2. Add the onion, shallot, and garlic, and sauté for 1–2 minutes, or until they begin to soften.
3. Add the salt, caraway seeds, pepper, cayenne, and paprika, and stir. Immediately remove from heat.
4. Add the onion mixture, potatoes, broth, and tomato paste to a 4-quart slow cooker. Stir to coat the potatoes evenly.
5. Cover and cook on high for 2½ hours, or until the potatoes are tender.
6. Turn off the heat and stir in the sour cream.

Potato Hot Pot

3 tablespoons olive oil, divided

1 large onion, diced

1 cup sliced mushrooms

5 cloves garlic, minced

⅛ teaspoon salt

⅛ teaspoon black pepper

¼ cup Earth Balance Original Buttery Spread

¼ cup flour

2 cups plain unsweetened soymilk

¼ cup nutritional yeast

1 tablespoon soy sauce

5 large potatoes, peeled and thinly sliced

1. Add 2 tablespoons of the olive oil to a sauté pan and sauté the onions, mushrooms, and garlic for 5 minutes. Add the salt and pepper to the mixture and set aside.
2. In another small saucepan, melt the Earth Balance and stir in the flour to make a roux.
3. Slowly add the soymilk until the sauce has thickened, stirring often. Mix in the nutritional yeast and soy sauce and set aside.
4. Grease the bottom of the slow cooker with the remaining 1 tablespoon olive oil and layer the potatoes.
5. Then, pour the onion and mushroom mixture on top of the potatoes.
6. Next, pour the nutritional yeast sauce on top of the mushroom mixture.
7. Cover the slow cooker and cook on low heat for 4 hours, or until the potatoes are tender.

Scalloped Potatoes

SERVES

8

4 large potatoes, thinly sliced

½ large white onion, julienned

2 cloves garlic, minced

3 cups Alfredo sauce

1 teaspoon salt

¼ teaspoon black pepper

½ cup water

1 teaspoon salt

Add all ingredients to a 4-quart slow cooker, cover, and cook on high heat for 4 hours.

Paella

SERVES

6

1 tablespoon olive oil

½ medium onion, diced

1 cup diced tomato

½ teaspoon saffron

1 teaspoon salt

2 tablespoons chopped fresh parsley

1 cup long-grain white rice

1 cup frozen peas

2 cups water

1 (12-ounce) package vegan chorizo, crumbled

1. Heat the olive oil in a sauté pan over medium heat. Add the onion and sauté for 3 minutes.
2. Add the tomato, saffron, salt, and parsley and stir.
3. Pour the sautéed mixture into a 4-quart slow cooker. Add the white rice, then frozen peas and water.
4. Cover and cook on low heat for 4 hours.
5. Pour the crumbled chorizo on top of the rice. Cover and cook for an additional 30 minutes. Stir before serving.

Tomatillo Rice

2 tablespoons olive oil

½ medium red onion, diced

½ red bell pepper, seeded and diced

2 cloves garlic, minced

1 lime, juiced

1 cup tomatillo salsa

1 cup water

1 teaspoon salt

1 cup long-grain white rice

½ cup chopped fresh cilantro

1. Heat the olive oil in a sauté pan over medium heat. Add the onion, bell pepper, and garlic, and sauté about 5 minutes.
2. Transfer to a 4-quart slow cooker. Add all the remaining ingredients except for the cilantro.
3. Cover and cook on high heat for 2½ hours. Check the rice periodically to make sure the liquid hasn't been absorbed too quickly and the rice is not drying out. If the rice is drying out too quickly, add ¼ cup of water.
4. Stir in the cilantro before serving.

Slow Cooker Suggestions

Tomatillos are small green tomatoes that are used in many Latin-inspired dishes. They come with a papery husk that surrounds the edible fruit. Try to find tomatillos with intact, tight-fitting, light brown husks; if the husk is dry or shriveled, the tomatillo is probably not good. Remove the husk before preparing.

Wild Mushroom Risotto

1 teaspoon olive oil

1 shallot, minced

2 cloves garlic, minced

8 ounces sliced button, shiitake, or oyster mushrooms

2 cups Arborio rice

2 cups Vegetable Broth (see recipe in Chapter 4), divided

3 cups water

$\frac{1}{2}$ teaspoon salt

1. Heat the oil over medium heat in a nonstick pan. Sauté the shallot, garlic, and mushrooms until soft, 4–5 minutes.
2. Add the rice and ½ cup Vegetable Broth, and cook until the liquid is fully absorbed, about 5 minutes.
3. Scrape the rice mixture into a 4-quart slow cooker. Add the water, salt, and remaining Vegetable Broth.
4. Cover and cook on low for 2 hours. Stir before serving.

Portobello Barley

1 teaspoon olive oil

2 shallots, minced

2 cloves garlic, minced

3 portobello mushroom caps, sliced

1 cup pearl barley

3¼ cups water

¼ teaspoon salt

½ teaspoon black pepper

1 teaspoon dried rosemary

1 teaspoon dried chervil

¼ cup grated Parmesan cheese

1. Heat the oil in a nonstick skillet over medium heat. Sauté the shallots, garlic, and mushrooms until softened, 3–4 minutes.
2. Place the mushroom mixture into a 4-quart slow cooker. Add the barley, water, salt, pepper, rosemary, and chervil. Stir.
3. Cover and cook on low for 8–9 hours or on high for 4 hours.
4. Turn off the slow cooker and stir in the Parmesan. Serve immediately.

Slow Cooker Suggestions

Chervil is an herb of the parsley family. It has delicate, curly leaves almost like carrot tops. Its mild flavor, which includes hints of anise, is easily overwhelmed by stronger flavors. Fresh parsley or tarragon, or a combination of both, can substitute for chervil.

Garlic-Pecan Brown Rice

SERVES

4

1 head garlic

1 tablespoon olive oil

½ cup finely chopped pecans

1 teaspoon dried parsley

¾ teaspoon salt

2 cups brown rice

3 cups water

1. Preheat the oven to 400°F. Cut the top ¼ off the head of garlic, place in aluminum foil, and drizzle with the olive oil.

2. Seal the aluminum foil at the top (like a small pouch) and cook for 30–45 minutes, or until soft.

3. Allow the garlic to cool completely, then remove each clove from the paper husk. Place all of the roasted garlic and all remaining ingredients in a 4-quart slow cooker.

4. Cover and cook on high heat for 2½–3 hours.

Slow Cooker Suggestions

Roasting garlic before using it in recipes brings out a whole new flavor. To enhance this dish even further, try toasting the pecans in a dry skillet for 3–4 minutes before adding to the slow cooker.

CHAPTER 7

Medleys and Main Dishes

Tofu Pepper Steak

1 (14-ounce) package extra-firm tofu, pressed and cut into strips

½ cup soy sauce, divided

3 tablespoons vegetable oil

1 green bell pepper, seeded and julienned

1 red bell pepper, seeded and julienned

1 medium onion, julienned

½ teaspoon red pepper flakes

1. In a small bowl, place the tofu and ¼ cup of soy sauce. Allow to marinate for 10 minutes.
2. In a 2-quart slow cooker, place tofu and add all remaining ingredients.
3. Cover and cook on low heat for 4 hours.

Slow Cooker Suggestions

To press tofu, line a plate with paper towels. Place the tofu block on the paper towels and put another layer of paper towels on top of the tofu. Put another plate on top of the paper towels and then weigh it down with heavy books. This releases any excess water in the tofu.

Ginger-Lime Tofu

2 (14-ounce) packages extra-firm tofu, pressed and sliced into fourths

¼ cup minced fresh ginger

¼ cup lime juice

1 lime, thinly sliced

1 small onion, thinly sliced

1. Place the tofu fillets in an oval 6- to 7-quart slow cooker.
2. Pour the ginger and lime juice over the tofu, then arrange the lime and then the onion in a single layer over the top.
3. Cook on low for 3–4 hours.

BBQ Tofu

2 (14-ounce) packages extra-firm tofu, pressed and crumbled

1 cup mustard

½ cup sugar

¾ cup apple cider vinegar

¼ cup water

2 tablespoons chili powder

½ teaspoon soy sauce

¼ teaspoon cayenne pepper

2 tablespoons butter or vegan margarine

1 tablespoon liquid smoke

½ teaspoon salt

⅛ teaspoon black pepper

1. Add all ingredients to a 4-quart slow cooker.
2. Cover and cook on low heat for 4 hours.

Slow Cooker Suggestions

To save a little bit of time and money, skip the homemade sauce in this recipe and use bottled barbecue sauce instead. Mix the bottled sauce with the tofu and cook. It's an easy process, and the results can still be delicious.

Classic Tofu "Stir-Fry"

1 red chili pepper, seeded and minced

2 cloves garlic, minced

1 teaspoon minced fresh ginger

1 tablespoon olive oil

3 tablespoons soy sauce

¼ cup water

1 tablespoon cornstarch

1 (14-ounce) package extra-firm tofu, pressed and cubed

2 tablespoons vegetable oil

2 large carrots, cut diagonally

1 red bell pepper, seeded and chopped

½ medium onion, sliced

2 cups chopped bok choy

½ cup chopped yellow squash

1. In a medium bowl, combine the chili pepper, garlic, ginger, olive oil, soy sauce, water, and cornstarch.
2. Pour the mixture over the tofu in a large bowl and allow to marinate for 10 minutes.
3. Add the rest of the ingredients to a 4-quart slow cooker. Add the tofu and the rest of the marinade.
4. Cover and cook on low heat for 4 hours.

Slow Cooker Suggestions

Cooking with cornstarch can be tricky. To make sure things go smoothly, always combine cornstarch with a liquid before adding it to dry ingredients in a recipe to avoid clumping.

Blackened Tofu

2 (14-ounce) packages extra-firm tofu, pressed and quartered

1/3 cup soy sauce

1 tablespoon apple cider vinegar

1 tablespoon minced garlic

1 tablespoon paprika

2 teaspoons black pepper

1 1/2 teaspoons salt

1 teaspoon garlic powder

1 teaspoon cayenne pepper

1/2 teaspoon dried oregano

1/2 teaspoon dried thyme

2 tablespoons vegetable oil

1. Place the tofu, soy sauce, vinegar, and garlic in a small bowl and allow to marinate for 10 minutes.

2. To make the blackened seasoning mixture, combine the paprika, black pepper, salt, garlic powder, cayenne, oregano, and thyme in a small bowl.

3. Remove the tofu from the soy marinade and dip each side into the blackened seasoning.

4. Add the oil and blackened tofu to a 2-quart slow cooker.

5. Cover and cook on low heat for 4 hours.

Slow Cooker Suggestions

Most major grocery stores carry two different types of tofu—regular or silken. Regular tofu is what you should always use unless the recipe specifically calls for silken, which is most common in desserts or recipes where the tofu needs a creamy consistency.

Maple-Glazed Tofu

4 cloves garlic, minced

1 tablespoon minced fresh ginger

½ cup maple syrup

¼ cup soy sauce

½ cup water

2 tablespoons brown sugar

1 lemon, juiced

¼ teaspoon black pepper

1 (14-ounce) package extra-firm tofu, pressed and quartered

1. In a large bowl, combine all the ingredients except for the tofu. Pour the mixture into a 4-quart slow cooker and add the tofu.
2. Set the slow cooker to high and cook for 1–2 hours, flipping the tofu at the halfway point.

Cracked-Pepper Tofu

6 cloves garlic, minced

¼ cup chopped fresh parsley

¼ cup chopped fresh rosemary

¼ cup rice vinegar

½ cup olive oil

¼ cup water

1 teaspoon black pepper

1 (14-ounce) package extra-firm tofu, pressed and quartered

1. In a large bowl, combine all the ingredients except for the tofu.
2. Pour the mixture into a 4-quart slow cooker and add the tofu.
3. Set the slow cooker to high and cook for 1–2 hours, flipping the tofu at the halfway point.

Broccoli, Snow Peas, and Seitan

SERVES
8

2 pounds seitan, cut into ½" strips

½ cup soy sauce

½ cup plus 1 teaspoon warm water, divided

1 tablespoon sesame oil

1 teaspoon sugar

2 cloves garlic, minced

1 teaspoon cornstarch

1 cup broccoli florets

1 cup snow peas

1. Place the seitan strips in a 4-quart slow cooker.
2. In a small bowl, whisk together the soy sauce, ½ cup water, sesame oil, sugar, and garlic, then pour over the seitan.
3. Cover and cook on low heat for 6 hours.
4. In a small bowl, whisk together the cornstarch and 1 teaspoon warm water, then add to the slow cooker, stirring until well combined.
5. Add the broccoli and snow peas.
6. Cover and cook for an additional 15 minutes.

Spiced Apple Cider Seitan

SERVES
8

3 pounds seitan, cubed

¼ teaspoon salt

¼ teaspoon black pepper

2 large apples, peeled, cored, and sliced

4 large sweet potatoes, peeled and cut in half

½ cup apple cider

½ teaspoon cinnamon

¼ teaspoon ground cloves

¼ teaspoon allspice

2 tablespoons brown sugar

1. Treat the crock of a 4-quart slow cooker with nonstick spray. Add seitan and season it with salt and pepper.

2. Arrange apple slices over and around the seitan, then add the sweet potatoes.

3. In a bowl or measuring cup, stir together the cider, cinnamon, cloves, allspice, and brown sugar. Pour over the ingredients in the slow cooker.

4. Cover and cook on low for 8 hours.

Seitan Cacciatore

2 tablespoons olive oil

1 (16-ounce) package seitan, cut into bite-sized pieces

1 large onion, chopped

1 red bell pepper, seeded and chopped

1 green bell pepper, seeded and chopped

4 cloves garlic, minced

1 (28-ounce) can diced tomatoes

1 cup Vegetable Broth (see recipe in Chapter 4)

2 tablespoons soy sauce

½ cup white wine

¼ teaspoon black pepper

2 tablespoons cornstarch, dissolved in 2 tablespoons water

¼ cup chopped fresh basil

1. Add the olive oil to a large sauté pan on medium heat and sauté the seitan for 3–5 minutes. Add the onion, bell peppers, and garlic, and sauté for an additional 3 minutes, then transfer to a 4-quart slow cooker.
2. Add the tomatoes, Vegetable Broth, soy sauce, white wine, and black pepper.
3. Cover and cook on low heat for 6 hours.
4. With a slotted spoon, remove the seitan from the slow cooker and set aside. Whisk in the cornstarch mixture until it creates a sauce consistency. Pour the sauce over the seitan. Garnish with the chopped basil before serving.

Slow Cooker Suggestions

If you'd like to leave the alcohol out of this dish, it's easy to substitute it with another liquid. Simply replace the wine with an additional ½ cup of Vegetable Broth.

Seitan Scaloppini

1 (16-ounce) package seitan, cut into 6 thin fillets

1 lemon, juiced

1 cup water

1 tablespoon Better Than Bouillon No Chicken Base

¼ cup white wine

¼ cup capers

¼ teaspoon black pepper

1 cup toasted panko bread crumbs

¼ cup chopped fresh parsley

1. Add the seitan, lemon juice, water, "chicken" base, white wine, capers, and black pepper to a 4-quart slow cooker.
2. Cover and cook on low heat for 4–6 hours.
3. Remove the seitan from the slow cooker and garnish with toasted bread crumbs and chopped parsley before serving.

Tempeh and Baby Bok Choy Scramble

1 (13-ounce) package tempeh, cut into bite-sized squares

3 heads baby bok choy, leaves cut into bite-sized pieces

1 medium onion, sliced

1 red pepper, seeded and chopped

3 cloves garlic, minced

1 cup vegetarian "chicken" broth

¼ teaspoon red pepper flakes

1 teaspoon salt

¼ teaspoon black pepper

1. Add all ingredients to a 4-quart slow cooker.
2. Cover and cook on low heat for 6 hours.

Carolina-Style Barbecue Tempeh

SERVES
4

4 cloves garlic, minced

2 teaspoons minced fresh ginger

1 cup soy sauce

½ cup apple cider vinegar

½ cup maple syrup

½ cup olive oil

2 teaspoons chipotle powder

1 teaspoon dried thyme

1 teaspoon paprika

1 teaspoon cumin

¼ teaspoon black pepper

1 (13-ounce) package tempeh, cut into bite-sized squares

4 hamburger buns

1. In a small bowl, combine all ingredients except for the tempeh and hamburger buns.
2. Add all ingredients, except for the hamburger buns, to a 4-quart slow cooker.
3. Cover and cook on low heat for 4 hours. Serve on the hamburger buns.

Tempeh Jambalaya

1 (13-ounce) package tempeh, cut into bite-sized squares

1 medium onion, chopped

2 stalks celery, chopped

1 bell pepper, seeded and chopped

4 cloves garlic, minced

2 cups white rice

2 teaspoons Better Than Bouillon No Chicken Base

5 cups water

1 (15-ounce) can tomato sauce

2 bay leaves

2 tablespoons Cajun seasoning

¼ teaspoon dried thyme

2 teaspoons hot sauce

1 teaspoon salt

¼ teaspoon black pepper

1. Add all ingredients to a 4-quart slow cooker.
2. Cover and cook on low heat for 6 hours or until all of the liquid is absorbed.

Slow Cooker Suggestions

There are two variations of jambalaya made throughout Louisiana—Creole and Cajun. The Creole version is tomato based, while the Cajun version omits the tomatoes in favor of more gamey meats, making it more difficult to transform into a vegetarian dish. This recipe strikes a balance between the two variations.

Tempeh and Greens

1 (13-ounce) package tempeh, cut into bite-sized squares

4 cloves garlic, minced

1 medium onion, chopped

8 cups stemmed and chopped collard greens

1 teaspoon Better Than Bouillon No Chicken Base

4 cups water

2 tablespoons soy sauce

1 teaspoon hot sauce

1 teaspoon salt

¼ teaspoon black pepper

1. Add all ingredients to a 4-quart slow cooker.
2. Cover and cook on low heat for 6 hours. Use a slotted spoon to serve the tempeh and greens in a bowl.

Tempeh and Gravy

SERVES 4

½ cup vegetable oil

3 cloves garlic, minced

¼ cup minced onion

½ cup flour

⅛ cup nutritional yeast

¼ cup soy sauce

2 cups water

½ teaspoon dried sage

¼ teaspoon black pepper

1 (13-ounce) package tempeh, cut into bite-sized squares

1. Add all ingredients, except for the tempeh, to a 4-quart slow cooker.
2. Cook on high heat for about 10 minutes, stirring continuously.
3. Add the tempeh, cover, and cook on low heat for 4 hours.

Slow Cooker Suggestions

Nutritional yeast, an inactive yeast, is a staple in many vegetarian kitchens. Because it is inactive, it won't make things rise and so should not be used for baking. It is often used to make cheese-style sauces due to its nutty, cheesy flavor. As a bonus, some brands are fortified with vitamin B_{12}.

CHAPTER 8

Roasts, Casseroles, and Other Comfort Foods

Simple Ratatouille

1 large onion, roughly chopped

1 eggplant, sliced horizontally

2 medium zucchini, sliced

1 cubanelle pepper, sliced

3 tomatoes, cut into wedges

2 tablespoons minced fresh basil

2 tablespoons minced fresh Italian parsley

¼ teaspoon salt

½ teaspoon black pepper

3 ounces tomato paste

¼ cup water

1. Place the onion, eggplant, zucchini, cubanelle pepper, and tomatoes into a 4-quart slow cooker.
2. Sprinkle with basil, parsley, salt, and black pepper.
3. In a small bowl, whisk the tomato paste and water together. Pour the mixture over the vegetables. Stir.
4. Cook on low for 4 hours, or until the eggplant and zucchini can easily be torn apart with a fork.

Slow Cooker Suggestions

Cubanelle peppers look very similar to banana peppers and are similar in taste and heat, but they are two different varieties. Cubanelles can be mild to somewhat spicy and, like banana peppers, are often pickled.

Tofu Roast

1 (14-ounce) package extra-firm tofu, pressed and quartered

4 tablespoons soy sauce

2 tablespoons olive oil

3 large potatoes, cubed

3 large carrots, chopped

1 medium onion, chopped

2 stalks celery, chopped

1 teaspoon salt

¼ teaspoon black pepper

1 tablespoon chopped fresh parsley

1. Place the tofu and soy sauce in a small bowl and allow to marinate for 10 minutes.

2. Add the rest of the ingredients, except for the parsley, to a 2-quart slow cooker.

3. Cover and cook on low heat for 4 hours. Add the parsley to the tofu roast.

Slow Cooker Suggestions

To achieve a more traditionally shaped roast, crumble the tofu, then shape into a loaf using a cheesecloth, pulling tightly to hold the tofu together and to remove excess liquid.

Mock Meatloaf

2 (14-ounce) packages extra-firm tofu, pressed and crumbled

¼ cup oats

¼ cup panko bread crumbs

½ cup ketchup, divided

1 teaspoon garlic powder

2 teaspoons vegan Worcestershire sauce, divided

½ large onion, diced

3 cloves garlic, minced

½ jalapeño, seeded and minced

½ teaspoon black pepper

1 tablespoon brown sugar

2 teaspoons ground mustard

1. In a large bowl, combine the tofu, oats, bread crumbs, 3 tablespoons ketchup, garlic powder, 1 teaspoon Worcestershire sauce, onion, garlic, jalapeño, and black pepper.
2. Press the mixture into the base of 2-quart slow cooker that has been prepped with cooking spray.
3. Cover and cook on low heat for 4–6 hours.
4. In a small bowl, combine the remaining ketchup and Worcestershire sauce, brown sugar, and mustard.
5. Pour the sauce on top of the "meatloaf" and continue cooking for 20 more minutes.

"Chicken" and Dumplings

SERVES

6

2 tablespoons vegetable oil

2 medium carrots, diced

2 stalks celery, diced

½ medium white onion, diced

1 cup frozen peas

1 pound seitan, cubed

2 (10½-ounce) cans cream of mushroom soup

2 teaspoons salt

½ teaspoon black pepper

½ teaspoon dried thyme

1 (10-ounce) package vegan biscuit dough

1. In a sauté pan over medium heat, add the vegetable oil, carrots, celery, and onion, and cook for 3–4 minutes until soft.

2. Transfer the cooked mixture to a 4-quart slow cooker. Add the frozen peas, seitan, soup, salt, pepper, and thyme.

3. Cover and cook over low heat for 6 hours.

4. Toward the end of the cooking time, tear each of the biscuits into fourths.

5. Remove the lid and drop in the biscuit dough piece by piece. Cover and cook for an additional 45 seconds.

Seitan Pot Pie

1 (16-ounce) package seitan, cut into bite-sized pieces

4 large red potatoes, quartered

2 medium carrots, chopped

½ cup chopped celery

½ cup sliced onions

2 (15-ounce) cans vegan cream of mushroom soup

2 teaspoons soy sauce

¼ teaspoon black pepper

1. Add all the ingredients to a 4-quart slow cooker.
2. Cover and cook on low heat for 6 hours.

Cheesy Seitan Pasta

1 teaspoon warm water

1 teaspoon cornstarch

3 cups 2% milk or unsweetened soymilk

2 cups Cheddar cheese

1 pound seitan, shredded

½ pound macaroni pasta

1. In a small bowl, whisk together the warm water and cornstarch.
2. Pour the cornstarch mixture into a 4-quart slow cooker, then add the milk, cheese, seitan, and macaroni.
3. Cover and cook on low heat for 6 hours.

Stroganoff

1 tablespoon extra-virgin olive oil

1 medium yellow onion, diced

2 cloves garlic, minced

1 pound seitan, chopped

1 teaspoon salt

4 cups Vegetable Broth (see recipe in Chapter 4)

½ cup vegan sour cream

1 tablespoon ground mustard

¼ cup chopped fresh parsley

1 pound cooked linguine or fettuccine pasta

1. Heat the olive oil in a sauté pan over medium heat. Add the onion and garlic, and cook for 2 minutes.
2. Place the sautéed onion and garlic, seitan, salt, and Vegetable Broth in a 4-quart slow cooker.
3. Cover and cook on low for 7 hours.
4. In a small bowl, combine the sour cream, mustard, and parsley. Add to the slow cooker, stirring well.
5. Cover and cook on low for an additional 15 minutes. Serve over cooked pasta.

Red Wine "Pot Roast"

⅓ cup red wine

½ cup water

4 medium red potatoes, quartered

3 medium carrots, cut into thirds

2 bulbs fennel, quartered

2 rutabagas, quartered

1 medium onion, sliced

4 cloves garlic, sliced

1½ pounds seitan, cubed

½ teaspoon salt

½ teaspoon black pepper

1. Pour the wine and water into a 4-quart slow cooker. Add the potatoes, carrots, fennel, rutabagas, onion, and garlic. Stir.
2. Add the seitan. Sprinkle with salt and pepper.
3. Cover and cook on low for 8 hours.

Braised Seitan with Mushrooms

1 cup sliced mushrooms

4 cups water

2 tablespoons Better Than Bouillon No Beef Base

½ cup red wine

1 teaspoon dried tarragon or thyme

1 teaspoon salt

¼ teaspoon black pepper

1 (16-ounce) package seitan, cut into bite-sized pieces

2 tablespoons cornstarch, dissolved in 2 tablespoons water

1. Add all of the ingredients, except for the cornstarch, to a 4-quart slow cooker. Cover and cook on low heat for 6 hours.
2. Use a slotted spoon to remove the seitan from the slow cooker and set aside.
3. Whisk in the cornstarch until it creates a gravy consistency, and then serve the mushroom gravy over the braised seitan.

Cottage Pie with Carrots, Parsnips, and Celery

SERVES 6

2 tablespoons olive oil

1 large onion, diced

3 cloves garlic, minced

1 large carrot, diced

1 parsnip, diced

1 stalk celery, diced

1 pound tempeh, crumbled

1½ cups Vegetable Broth (see recipe in Chapter 4)

½ teaspoon hot paprika

½ teaspoon dried rosemary

1 tablespoon vegan Worcestershire sauce

½ teaspoon dried savory

⅛ teaspoon salt

¼ teaspoon black pepper

1 tablespoon cornstarch, dissolved in 1 tablespoon water, if needed

¼ cup minced fresh parsley

2¾ cups cooked potatoes

1. Place the olive oil in a large sauté pan over medium heat. Sauté the onions, garlic, carrots, parsnips, celery, and tempeh for about 5 minutes.

2. Place the mixture into a round 4-quart slow cooker. Add the Vegetable Broth, paprika, rosemary, Worcestershire sauce, savory, salt, and pepper. Stir.

3. Cook on low for 6–8 hours. If the meat mixture still looks very wet, add the cornstarch. Stir this into the slow cooker.

4. In a medium bowl, mash the parsley and potatoes using a potato masher. Spread on top of the tempeh mixture in the slow cooker.

5. Cover and cook on high for 30–60 minutes, or until the potatoes are warmed through.

Slow Cooker Suggestions

Take a few minutes the night before cooking to cut up any vegetables you'll need for a recipe the next day. Place them in an airtight container or plastic bag and refrigerate until morning. Measure any dried spices and place them in a small container on the counter until needed.

"Short Rib" Tempeh

1 (13-ounce) package tempeh, cut into strips

1 (28-ounce) can tomato sauce

½ cup water

2 tablespoons vegan Worcestershire sauce

2 tablespoons brown sugar

2 tablespoons dried parsley

1 teaspoon Tabasco sauce

¼ teaspoon black pepper

1 lemon, juiced

1 tablespoon soy sauce

1. Add all ingredients to a 4-quart slow cooker.
2. Cover and cook on low heat for 6 hours.

Tempeh Pot Pie

½ cup Earth Balance Original Buttery Spread

1 large onion, chopped

2 large carrots, chopped

1 cup chopped mushrooms

½ cup flour

1 cup unsweetened soymilk

1 cup frozen peas

1 (13-ounce) package tempeh, cut into bite-sized squares

½ cup water

2 teaspoons lemon pepper

1 teaspoon salt

¼ teaspoon black pepper

1 sheet frozen puff pastry, cut into 4 squares

1. Add the Earth Balance to a large sauté pan over medium heat. Once melted, add the onion, carrots, and mushrooms, and sauté for 3–5 minutes.
2. Add the flour and whisk to create a roux, then slowly whisk in the soymilk and stir until all lumps have been removed.
3. Transfer the contents of the sauté pan to a 4-quart slow cooker and add all remaining ingredients, except for the puff pastry.
4. Cover and cook on low heat for 6 hours.
5. Meanwhile, cook the puff pastry according to package directions, or until it is golden brown. Serve the pot pie in a bowl and top each bowl with one square of the puff pastry.

Lemon-Pepper Tempeh

1 (13-ounce) package tempeh, cut into bite-sized squares

6 cloves garlic, minced

1 teaspoon minced fresh ginger

¾ cup water

¼ cup soy sauce

½ cup extra-virgin olive oil

¼ cup fresh lemon juice

1 teaspoon black pepper

1. Add all ingredients to a 4-quart slow cooker.
2. Cover and cook on low heat for 6 hours.

CHAPTER 9

Sandwiches

Tofu Salad Sub

¼ cup olive oil

1 tablespoon lemon juice

½ teaspoon salt

½ teaspoon black pepper

1 clove garlic, minced

¼ cup diced celery

2 teaspoons dried dill

1 (14-ounce) package extra-firm tofu, pressed and crumbled

4 hoagie rolls

1. In a small bowl, whisk together the olive oil, lemon juice, salt, pepper, garlic, celery, and dill.
2. Place the crumbled tofu in the bottom of a 2-quart slow cooker, then top with the olive oil and lemon juice blend.
3. Cover and cook on low heat for 2 hours.
4. Place ¼ of the cooked tofu on each of the hoagie rolls, dress with your favorite toppings, and serve.

Cajun Tempeh Po' Boys

1 (13-ounce) package tempeh, cut into small
    bite-sized squares

½ cup olive oil

5 cloves garlic, minced

1 large onion, chopped

2 teaspoons dried oregano

2 teaspoons dried thyme

2 teaspoons cayenne pepper

2 tablespoons paprika

1 teaspoon salt

¼ teaspoon black pepper

1 loaf French bread, sliced horizontally

2 cups shredded lettuce

2 tomatoes, sliced

1. Add all ingredients, except for the bread, lettuce, and tomatoes, to a
   4-quart slow cooker.
2. Cover and cook on high heat for 2 hours.
3. Assemble the sandwiches on the bread by layering the tempeh,
   lettuce, and tomatoes.

Seitan Sandwich Meat

SERVES 8

4 cups Vegetable Broth (see recipe in Chapter 4)

1 teaspoon salt

2 teaspoons black pepper

2 teaspoons garlic powder

2 teaspoons onion powder

1 teaspoon dried oregano

1 teaspoon soy sauce

1 teaspoon liquid smoke

2 pounds seitan, divided into 2 large pieces

1. Combine all ingredients except for the seitan in a 4-quart slow cooker, stirring well.
2. Add the seitan. Cover and cook on low heat for 6 hours.
3. Remove the seitan from the liquid and, once cool, slice into thin sandwich slices.

Slow Cooker Suggestions

Spice up this recipe by adding a teaspoon of cayenne or chipotle pepper. Another recipe variation is to make it more Italian by omitting soy sauce and adding a handful of fresh basil instead.

Seitan Po' Boys

3 tablespoons olive oil

1 (16-ounce) package seitan, cut into bite-sized pieces

½ cup water

2 tablespoons Old Bay seasoning

1 teaspoon salt

¼ teaspoon black pepper

6 French bread rolls

2 cups shredded lettuce

1 tomato, sliced

16 dill pickle slices

¼ cup mayonnaise or vegan mayonnaise

1. Add olive oil, seitan, water, Old Bay, salt, and pepper to a 4-quart slow cooker.
2. Cover and cook on high heat for 1 hour.
3. Serve seitan on French bread rolls with lettuce, tomato, pickle, and mayonnaise.

French Dip Seitan Sandwiches

1 (16-ounce) package seitan, thinly sliced

2 quarts vegetarian "beef" broth

8–12 pieces sliced bread

1. Add the seitan and broth to a 4-quart slow cooker.
2. Cover and cook on high heat for 2 hours.
3. Place the seitan on the bread and assemble the French dip sandwiches. Serve the extra broth in ramekins for dipping.

Seitan Cuban Sandwich

1 (16-ounce) package seitan, thinly sliced

6 oranges, juiced

6 limes, juiced

½ teaspoon cumin

1 teaspoon dried oregano

½ teaspoon lemon pepper

2 tablespoons soy sauce

¼ cup olive oil

1 loaf Cuban bread, sliced in half

4 slices vegan pepper jack cheese

12 dill pickle slices

4 teaspoons mustard

1. Add all of the ingredients, except for the bread, cheese, pickles, and mustard, to a 4-quart slow cooker.
2. Cover and cook the seitan on high heat for 1–2 hours.
3. Remove the slices of seitan with tongs and assemble the sandwiches on the bread by layering the seitan, cheese, pickles, and mustard.

Tempeh Reuben Sandwiches

1 (13-ounce) package tempeh, cut into strips

1 cup water

¼ cup apple cider vinegar

2 tablespoons paprika

1 tablespoon dried oregano

¼ cup Dijon mustard

¼ teaspoon liquid smoke

2 teaspoons allspice

3 cloves garlic, minced

1 teaspoon salt

¼ teaspoon black pepper

12 slices rye bread

1 cup sauerkraut

6 slices Swiss cheese

½ cup Thousand Island dressing

1. Add the tempeh, water, apple cider vinegar, paprika, oregano, Dijon mustard, liquid smoke, allspice, garlic, salt, and pepper to a 4-quart slow cooker.
2. Cover and cook on low heat for 4 hours.
3. Serve on the rye bread with sauerkraut, cheese, and Thousand Island dressing.

Tempeh Sliders

1 (13-ounce) package tempeh cut into 8 squares

2 cloves garlic, minced

1 teaspoon minced fresh ginger

¼ cup soy sauce

1 cup water

¼ teaspoon black pepper

½ teaspoon garlic powder

½ teaspoon onion powder

¼ teaspoon cumin

⅛ teaspoon cayenne pepper

2 teaspoons olive oil

½ large onion, sliced

8 slices Cheddar cheese

8 mini sandwich buns

1. Add the tempeh, garlic, ginger, soy sauce, water, black pepper, garlic powder, onion powder, cumin, and cayenne pepper to a 4-quart slow cooker.
2. Cover and cook on low heat for 6 hours.
3. About 5 minutes before the tempeh is done cooking, add the olive oil to a pan and sauté the onions over medium-high heat until they are soft, about 5 minutes.
4. Melt a slice of cheese on each piece of tempeh and top with the onions. Serve on mini sandwich buns.

CHAPTER 10

Asian-Inspired Dishes

Pho

1 tablespoon coriander seeds

1 tablespoon whole cloves

6 star anise

1 cinnamon stick

1 tablespoon fennel seed

1 tablespoon whole cardamom

4 knobs fresh ginger, sliced

1 small onion, sliced

4 cups Vegetable Broth (see recipe in Chapter 4)

1 teaspoon soy sauce

8 ounces Vietnamese rice noodles

1 cup shredded seitan

½ cup chopped fresh cilantro

½ cup chopped fresh Thai basil

2 cups mung bean sprouts

¼ cup sliced scallions

1. In a dry nonstick skillet, quickly heat the coriander, cloves, anise, cinnamon, fennel, cardamom, ginger, and onion over high heat until the seeds start to pop, about 5 minutes. The onion and ginger should look slightly caramelized.
2. Place the spices, ginger, and onion in a cheesecloth packet and tie it securely.
3. Place the cheesecloth packet in a 4-quart slow cooker. Add the broth, soy sauce, noodles, and seitan.
4. Cover and cook on low for 4 hours.
5. Remove the cheesecloth packet after cooking. Serve each bowl topped with cilantro, basil, sprouts, and scallions.

Korean-Style Hot Pot

3 bunches baby bok choy

8 cups water

8 ounces sliced cremini mushrooms

1 (12-ounce) package extra-firm tofu, pressed and cubed

3 cloves garlic, thinly sliced

¼ teaspoon sesame oil

1 tablespoon red pepper flakes

7 ounces enoki mushrooms

1. Remove the leaves of the baby bok choy. Wash thoroughly.
2. Place the whole leaves in a 4-quart slow cooker. Add the water, cremini mushrooms, tofu, garlic, sesame oil, and red pepper flakes. Stir.
3. Cook on low for 8 hours.
4. Add the enoki mushrooms and stir. Cook an additional 30 minutes.

Curried Cauliflower

1 tablespoon olive oil

¼ cup finely diced onion

1½ teaspoons curry powder

½ teaspoon cumin

½ teaspoon coriander

1 teaspoon chili powder

1 teaspoon salt

1 cup diced tomatoes

1 cup water

1 head cauliflower, chopped

1. Heat the olive oil in the bottom of a 4-quart slow cooker set to high heat. Add the onion and cook for 5 minutes.
2. Add the curry powder, cumin, coriander, chili powder, salt, and tomatoes, and stir until well combined.
3. Add the water and cauliflower to the spice mixture in the slow cooker and stir until the cauliflower is coated.
4. Cover and cook over low heat for about 4 hours.

Sesame Adzuki Beans

1 (16-ounce) bag dried adzuki beans

Water, enough to cover beans by 1"

1 teaspoon salt

1 tablespoon sesame oil

1 tablespoon soy sauce

1 teaspoon rice wine vinegar

2 teaspoons toasted sesame seeds

1. Add the adzuki beans, water, and salt to a 4-quart slow cooker.
2. Cover and cook on low heat for 6 hours. Check the beans at about 5 hours to see if they are tender and continue cooking if necessary.
3. Once the beans are done, drain in a colander and allow to cool.
4. Pour the beans into a bowl and stir in the sesame oil, soy sauce, rice wine vinegar, and sesame seeds.

Chana Masala

2 (15-ounce) cans chickpeas, drained

1 cup water

4 teaspoons salt

¼ cup Earth Balance Original Buttery Spread

1 medium onion, diced

5 cloves garlic, minced

1 tablespoon cumin

½ teaspoon cayenne pepper

1 teaspoon turmeric

2 teaspoons paprika

1 teaspoon garam masala

1 cup diced tomatoes

1 lemon, juiced

2 teaspoons grated fresh ginger

1. Add all ingredients to a 4-quart slow cooker.
2. Cover and cook on low heat for 6 hours.

Sweet and Sour Tofu

SERVES 6

1 (12-ounce) package extra-firm tofu, pressed and cubed

¼ cup rice vinegar

3 tablespoons water

1 tablespoon sesame seeds

1 tablespoon brown sugar

1 tablespoon tamari

1 tablespoon pineapple juice

1 teaspoon ground ginger

¾ cup pineapple chunks

1 cup snow peas

½ cup sliced onion

1. Spray a nonstick skillet with cooking spray. Sauté the tofu until it is lightly browned on each side. Add to a 4-quart slow cooker.

2. In a small bowl, whisk together the vinegar, water, sesame seeds, brown sugar, tamari, pineapple juice, and ginger until the sugar fully dissolves. Pour over the tofu. Add the remaining ingredients.

3. Cover and cook on low for 4 hours. Remove the lid and cook on low for 30 minutes.

Slow Cooker Suggestions

For added texture, try breading the cubed tofu with flour or panko bread crumbs and then pan-frying it in 2 tablespoons of oil. You can then proceed with the remainder of the recipe.

Kung Pao Tofu

2 tablespoons white wine

2 tablespoons soy sauce

2 tablespoons sesame oil

2 tablespoons cornstarch, dissolved in 2 tablespoons water

½ tablespoon hot chili paste

1 teaspoon rice wine vinegar

2 teaspoons brown sugar

1 (14-ounce) package extra-firm tofu, pressed and cubed

½ cup water

1 teaspoon olive oil

½ red bell pepper, seeded and chopped

1 clove garlic, minced

¼ cup peanuts

1. In a medium bowl, combine the white wine, soy sauce, sesame oil, cornstarch, chili paste, rice wine vinegar, and brown sugar.
2. Pour the mixture over the tofu and allow to marinate for 10 minutes.
3. Add all ingredients, except for the peanuts, to a 4-quart slow cooker.
4. Cover and cook on low heat for 4 hours.
5. Add the peanuts before serving.

Palak Tofu

1 (14-ounce) package extra-firm tofu, pressed

1 tablespoon canola oil

1 teaspoon cumin seeds

2 cloves garlic, minced

2 jalapeños, seeded and minced

¾ pound red potatoes, diced

½ teaspoon ground ginger

¾ teaspoon garam masala

1 pound frozen cut-leaf spinach

¼ cup chopped fresh cilantro

1. Cut the tofu into ½" cubes. Set aside.
2. Heat the oil in a nonstick skillet. Add the cumin seeds and sauté for 1 minute.
3. Add the garlic and jalapeños. Sauté until fragrant, about 1 minute.
4. Add the tofu and potatoes. Sauté for 3 minutes.
5. Now put in the ginger, garam masala, frozen spinach, and cilantro. Sauté 1 minute.
6. Pour the mixture into a 4-quart slow cooker and cook for 4 hours on low.

Slow Cooker Suggestions

There are many different ways to enjoy Indian dishes such as this one. Try it over a bed of jasmine rice, scoop it up with naan (Indian flatbread), or roll it up in chapati (another type of flatbread).

Thai Tofu Coconut Curry

1 (12-ounce) package extra-firm tofu, pressed

¼ cup unsweetened shredded coconut

¼ cup water

4 cloves garlic, minced

1 tablespoon minced fresh ginger

1 tablespoon minced galangal root

½ cup chopped onion

1 cup peeled and diced sweet potato

1 cup broccoli florets

1 cup snow peas

3 tablespoons tamari

1 tablespoon vegetarian fish sauce

1 tablespoon chili-garlic sauce

½ cup minced fresh cilantro

½ cup light coconut milk

1. Slice the tofu into ½"-thick triangles.
2. Place the tofu into a 4-quart slow cooker. Top with coconut, water, garlic, ginger, galangal, onion, sweet potato, broccoli, snow peas, tamari, vegetarian fish sauce, and chili-garlic sauce.
3. Stir to distribute all ingredients evenly. Cook on low for 5 hours.
4. Stir in the cilantro and coconut milk. Cook on low for an additional 20 minutes. Stir prior to serving.

Panang Tofu

1 (14-ounce) package extra-firm tofu, pressed and cubed

1 (13-ounce) can coconut milk

1 tablespoon Panang curry paste

2 tablespoons soy sauce

1 tablespoon lime juice

2 tablespoons sugar

2 tablespoons olive oil

¼ medium onion, sliced

½ medium carrot, sliced diagonally

½ red bell pepper, seeded and chopped

½ cup chopped fresh basil

1. Add all ingredients, except for the basil, to a 4-quart slow cooker.
2. Cover and cook on low heat for 4–6 hours.
3. Add the basil before serving.

Peanut and Sesame Sauce Tofu

4 cloves garlic, minced

1 tablespoon minced fresh ginger

1 cup creamy peanut butter

1 cup coconut milk

¼ cup unsweetened soymilk

2 tablespoons soy sauce

1 lime, juiced

1 (14-ounce) package extra-firm tofu, pressed and
   cut into 1" cubes

1. In a large bowl, combine all the ingredients except for the tofu.
2. Pour the mixture into a 4-quart slow cooker and add the tofu.
3. Set the slow cooker to high and cook for 1–2 hours, flipping the tofu
   at the halfway point.

Slow Cooker Suggestions

There are endless options for serving Asian-style tofu. Try this tofu as
the filling for lettuce wraps, over rice noodles, or as the protein on a
tasty kebab. You can also play it safe and serve this dish over a bed
of steamed rice.

Indian Spinach and Tofu

SERVES 4

2 tablespoons olive oil

4 cloves garlic, minced

1 teaspoon minced fresh ginger

1 cup frozen spinach, thawed and drained

1 tablespoon cumin

1 tablespoon coriander

1 teaspoon turmeric

½ teaspoon red pepper flakes

¼ teaspoon mustard seeds

1 (15-ounce) can coconut milk

¼ cup soy sauce

1 (14-ounce) package extra-firm tofu, pressed and quartered

1. Add the olive oil to a sauté pan and sauté the garlic and ginger on medium-high heat for 1 minute.
2. Add this mixture to a 4-quart slow cooker, then mix in the spinach, cumin, coriander, turmeric, red pepper flakes, mustard seeds, coconut milk, and soy sauce.
3. Add the tofu, set the slow cooker to high, and cook for 1–2 hours, flipping the tofu at the halfway point.

Cashew Seitan

¼ cup rice wine

½ cup hoisin sauce

¼ cup soy sauce

½ cup water

1 tablespoon sugar

2 tablespoons olive oil

1 red bell pepper, seeded and chopped

1 green bell pepper, seeded and chopped

4 cloves garlic, minced

1 (16-ounce) package seitan, cut into bite-sized pieces

½ cup cashew pieces

1. Combine the rice wine, hoisin, soy sauce, water, and sugar in a 4-quart slow cooker.
2. Stir well, and then add all remaining ingredients except for the cashews.
3. Cover and cook on low for 6 hours. Garnish with cashew pieces before serving.

Mandarin Seitan

4 cloves garlic, minced

1 teaspoon minced fresh ginger

1 (16-ounce) package seitan, cut into bite-sized pieces

½ cup soy sauce

⅓ cup sugar

1 lemon, juiced

1 cup water

2 tablespoons cornstarch, dissolved in 2 tablespoons water

1. Add all of the ingredients, except for the cornstarch, to a 4-quart slow cooker.
2. Cover and cook on high for 2 hours.
3. Remove the seitan with a slotted spoon. Whisk in the cornstarch until the liquid has the consistency of a sauce.

Orange Wasabi Soy Tempeh

2 cups orange juice

1 cup agave nectar

½ cup soy sauce

2 limes, juiced

½ teaspoon wasabi powder

1 cup water

1 (13-ounce) package tempeh, cut into bite-sized squares

1. In a medium bowl, combine all ingredients except for the tempeh.
2. Put the tempeh in a 4-quart slow-cooker and pour the liquid mixture over it.
3. Cover and cook on low heat for 4 hours.

Ginger-Soy Tempeh Cubes

3 cloves garlic, minced

1 tablespoon minced fresh ginger

½ cup soy sauce

1 cup water

2 limes, juiced

¼ cup olive oil

2 tablespoons sugar

1 (13-ounce) package tempeh, cut into bite-sized squares

3 green onions, sliced

1. In a small bowl, combine garlic, ginger, soy sauce, water, lime juice, olive oil, and sugar.
2. Add the garlic mixture and tempeh to a 4-quart slow cooker.
3. Cover and cook on low heat for 4 hours. Garnish with the green onions.

Sriracha and Soy Tempeh

1 (13-ounce) package tempeh, cut into bite-sized squares

4 cloves garlic, minced

1 teaspoon minced fresh ginger

1 tablespoon olive oil

½ cup soy sauce

¼ cup water

2 tablespoons brown sugar

1 teaspoon sriracha sauce

1. Add all ingredients to a 4-quart slow cooker.
2. Cover and cook on high heat for 2 hours.

Indian Curry Tempeh

1 (13-ounce) package tempeh, cut into
   bite-sized squares

3 cloves garlic, minced

1 teaspoon minced fresh ginger

1 large onion, sliced

2 large carrots, julienned

1 cup chopped cauliflower

1/3 cup tomato paste

1 (15-ounce) can coconut milk

1 cup water

1/4 cup curry powder

1 (15-ounce) can chickpeas, drained

1 teaspoon salt

1/4 teaspoon black pepper

1. Add all ingredients to a 4-quart slow cooker.
2. Cover and cook on low heat for 4 hours.

General Tso's Tempeh

4 cloves garlic, minced

3 teaspoons minced fresh ginger

¾ cup soy sauce

2 tablespoons cornstarch

1 cup boiling water

¼ cup sugar

2 tablespoons white wine vinegar

2 tablespoons sherry

2 teaspoons red pepper flakes

2 cups chopped broccoli

2 medium carrots, sliced

1 (13-ounce) package tempeh, cut into bite-sized pieces

1. In a medium bowl, combine the garlic, ginger, soy sauce, cornstarch, water, sugar, vinegar, sherry, and red pepper flakes.
2. Add all ingredients to a 4-quart slow cooker.
3. Cover and cook on low heat for 4 hours.

CHAPTER 11

International Favorites

Greek-Style Orzo and Spinach Soup

2 cloves garlic, minced

3 tablespoons lemon juice

1 teaspoon lemon zest

5 cups Vegetable Broth (see recipe in Chapter 4)

1½ teaspoons salt

1 small onion, thinly sliced

1 (14-ounce) package extra-firm tofu, pressed and cubed

4 cups fresh baby spinach

⅓ cup dried orzo

1. In a 4-quart slow cooker, add the garlic, lemon juice, zest, broth, salt, onion, tofu, and spinach.
2. Cover and cook on low for 1 hour.
3. Add the orzo, stir, and continue to cook on high for an additional 15 minutes. Stir before serving.

Slow Cooker Suggestions

There are many tools on the market for zesting citrus, but all you really need is a fine grater. Be sure to grate off only the outermost part of the peel, because this is where the aromatic essential oils that hold the flavor are located. The white pith underneath is bitter and inedible.

Posole

8 large dried New Mexican red chilies

1½ quarts Vegetable Broth (see recipe in Chapter 4), divided

3 cloves garlic, minced

2 tablespoons lime juice

1 tablespoon cumin

1 tablespoon dried oregano

1 (7-ounce) package Gardein Chick'n Strips

¾ cup flour

1 teaspoon canola oil

1 large onion, sliced

40 ounces canned hominy

1. Seed the chilies, reserving the seeds.
2. In a dry, hot frying pan, heat the chilies until warmed through and fragrant, 2–3 minutes. Do not burn or brown them.
3. In a medium pot, place the chilies and seeds, 1 quart broth, garlic, lime juice, cumin, and oregano. Bring to a boil and continue to boil for 20 minutes.
4. Meanwhile, in a plastic bag, toss the Chick'n Strips with the flour to coat. Heat the oil in a large nonstick skillet and brown the vegan meat on all sides, about 3 minutes.
5. Add the onions and cook about 5 minutes, or until the onions are soft.
6. In a 4-quart slow cooker, pour in the remaining broth, the onion and Chick'n Strips mixture, and the hominy.
7. Strain the chili-stock mixture through a mesh sieve and pour into the slow cooker insert, mashing down with a wooden spoon to press out the pulp and juice. Discard the seeds and remaining solids.
8. Cook on low for 8 hours.

Slow Cooker Suggestions

If you have a small amount of juice left from a lemon or lime, pour it into an ice cube freezer tray, one well at a time, and then freeze. Leftover zest can also be saved. Place the zest in a freezer bag and refrigerate for up to 1 week, or freeze it in a freezer-safe container for up to 1 month.

Moroccan Root Vegetables

1 pound parsnips, peeled and diced

1 pound turnips, peeled and diced

2 medium onions, chopped

1 pound carrots, diced

6 dried apricots, chopped

4 pitted prunes, chopped

1 teaspoon turmeric

1 teaspoon cumin

½ teaspoon ground ginger

½ teaspoon cinnamon

¼ teaspoon cayenne pepper

1 tablespoon dried parsley

1 tablespoon dried cilantro

2 cups Vegetable Broth (see recipe in Chapter 4)

1 teaspoon salt

1. Add the parsnips, turnips, onions, carrots, apricots, prunes, turmeric, cumin, ginger, cinnamon, cayenne pepper, parsley, and cilantro to a 4-quart slow cooker.
2. Pour in the Vegetable Broth and salt.
3. Cover and cook on low for 9 hours, or until the vegetables are cooked through.

Artichoke Barigoule

SERVES
6

6 whole artichoke hearts, quartered

2 medium carrots, finely diced

2 shallots, finely diced

3 cloves garlic, minced

2 lemons, juiced

½ cup white wine

½ cup water

¼ cup olive oil

1 sprig fresh thyme, chopped

½ teaspoon salt

¼ cup chopped fresh flat-leaf parsley

1. In a 2-quart slow cooker, place all ingredients except for the parsley. Stir well and cover.
2. Cook on low heat for 4 hours.
3. Stir in the chopped parsley and serve.

Slow Cooker Suggestions

Barigoule is a traditional Provençal dish, which means it hails from the Provence region in the south of France. The cuisine of Provence is influenced by the region's proximity to the Mediterranean Sea, and Provençal dishes are characterized by the use of seafood, olives, and garlic.

Tofu with Lemon, Capers, and Rosemary

SERVES 4

1 (14-ounce) package extra-firm tofu, pressed and sliced into quarters

⅓ cup water

2 tablespoons lemon juice

½ teaspoon salt

3 thin slices fresh lemon

1 tablespoon nonpareil capers

½ teaspoon minced fresh rosemary

1. Place the tofu fillets on the bottom of a 2-quart slow cooker.
2. Pour the water, lemon juice, and salt over the tofu.
3. Arrange the lemon slices in a single layer on top of the tofu. Sprinkle with capers and rosemary.
4. Cover and cook on low for 2 hours. Discard lemon slices prior to serving.

Middle Eastern Lemon Seitan

SERVES 6

1 lemon, juiced

1 (15-ounce) can diced tomatoes

1 (15-ounce) can chickpeas, drained

½ cup water

1 teaspoon cumin

1 teaspoon coriander

4 cloves garlic, minced

½ teaspoon cinnamon

½ teaspoon salt

1 (16-ounce) package seitan, cut into bite-sized pieces

1. Add all of the ingredients to a 4-quart slow cooker.
2. Cover and cook on low heat for 6 hours.

Moroccan "Chicken"

½ teaspoon coriander

½ teaspoon cinnamon

¼ teaspoon salt

1 teaspoon cumin

2 pounds seitan, cubed

½ cup water

4 cloves garlic, minced

1 small onion, thinly sliced

1 knob ginger, minced

1 (15-ounce) can chickpeas, drained and rinsed

4 ounces dried apricots, halved

1. Place all of the spices, seitan, water, garlic, onion, and ginger into a 4-quart slow cooker. Cook on low for 5 hours.
2. Stir in the chickpeas and apricots and cook on high for 40 minutes.

Seitan Provençal

1 (16-ounce) package seitan, cut into bite-sized pieces

1 (28-ounce) can diced tomatoes

½ cup white wine

1 cup Vegetable Broth (see recipe in Chapter 4)

4 cloves garlic, minced

¼ cup pitted and chopped kalamata olives

1 teaspoon salt

¼ teaspoon black pepper

¼ cup chopped fresh basil

1. Add all ingredients, except for the basil, to a 4-quart slow cooker. Cover and cook on low heat for 6 hours.
2. Sprinkle with basil just before serving.

Spicy Seitan Tacos

2 tablespoons olive oil

1 (16-ounce) package seitan, chopped into small pieces

2 cloves garlic, minced

½ cup soy sauce

1 tablespoon chili powder

¼ teaspoon chipotle powder

¼ teaspoon garlic powder

¼ teaspoon red pepper flakes

¼ teaspoon onion powder

2 teaspoons cumin

½ teaspoon paprika

1 teaspoon black pepper

8 taco shells

1 cup shredded lettuce

1 tomato, diced

1. Add all the ingredients, except for shells, lettuce, and tomatoes, to a 4-quart slow cooker.
2. Cover and cook on low heat for 4 hours.
3. Serve the seitan in the shells and top with lettuce and tomato.

Jerk Seitan

1 pound shredded seitan

½ cup Vegetable Broth (see recipe in Chapter 4)

½ teaspoon allspice

¼ teaspoon cinnamon

½ teaspoon dried thyme

¼ teaspoon nutmeg

1 teaspoon salt

¼ cup diced red onion

2 cloves garlic, minced

2 tablespoons seeded and minced jalapeño

1. Prepare a 4-quart slow cooker with nonstick cooking spray, then add the shredded seitan.

2. In a medium bowl, combine all remaining ingredients. Pour over the seitan.

3. Cover and cook on low for 6 hours.

Vegan Ropa Vieja

2 pounds cubed seitan

1 cubanelle pepper, diced

1 large onion, diced

2 large carrots, diced

2 (15-ounce) cans canned crushed tomatoes

2 cloves garlic, minced

1 teaspoon dried oregano

½ teaspoon cumin

½ cup sliced green olives stuffed with pimento

1. Add all of the ingredients to a 4-quart slow cooker.
2. Cook on low for 7 hours.
3. Shred the seitan with a fork, knife, or grater, then mash it with a potato masher until very well mixed.

Italian Herb Seitan

1 (16-ounce) package seitan, cut into bite-sized pieces

6 cloves garlic, minced

¼ cup rice wine vinegar

½ cup Vegetable Broth (see recipe in Chapter 4)

½ cup chopped fresh rosemary

½ cup chopped fresh parsley

1 teaspoon salt

¼ teaspoon black pepper

1. Add all of the ingredients to a 4-quart slow cooker.
2. Cover and cook on low heat for 6 hours.

Italian Tempeh with Cannellini Beans

1½ pounds tempeh, sliced into 1" strips

1 (28-ounce) can crushed tomatoes

1 head roasted garlic

1 large onion, minced

2 tablespoons capers

2 teaspoons Italian-blend herbs

1 (15-ounce) can cannellini beans, drained and rinsed

1. Place the tempeh into a 4-quart slow cooker. Add the tomatoes, garlic, onions, capers, and Italian-blend herbs.
2. Cover and cook on low for 7–8 hours.
3. Add the cannellini beans 1 hour before serving and continue to cook on low for the remaining time.

Spicy Tempeh Fajitas

1 (13-ounce) package tempeh, cut into bite-sized pieces

2 cloves garlic, minced

1 teaspoon minced fresh ginger

¼ cup soy sauce

1 cup water

1 tablespoon olive oil

½ teaspoon chili powder

¼ teaspoon chipotle powder

¼ teaspoon black pepper

½ medium onion, sliced

½ green bell pepper, seeded and sliced

1 jalapeño, seeded and minced

½ cup sliced mushrooms

12 corn tortillas

1 tomato, diced

¼ cup chopped fresh cilantro

1 lime, cut into wedges

1. Add the tempeh, garlic, ginger, soy sauce, water, olive oil, chili powder, chipotle powder, black pepper, onion, green bell pepper, jalapeño, and mushrooms to a 4-quart slow cooker.
2. Cover and cook on low heat for 6 hours.
3. Serve the fajitas on the tortillas and garnish with tomato, cilantro, and lime.

Tempeh Tamale Pie

2 tablespoons olive oil

1 large onion, minced

1 pound tempeh, crumbled

1 jalapeño, seeded and minced

2 cloves garlic, minced

1 (15-ounce) can diced tomatoes

1 (10-ounce) can diced tomatoes with green chilies

1 (15-ounce) can dark red kidney beans, drained and rinsed

4 chipotle peppers in adobo, minced

½ teaspoon hot Mexican chili powder

⅔ cup unsweetened soymilk

2 tablespoons canola oil

2 teaspoons baking powder

½ cup cornmeal

½ teaspoon salt

1. In a large sauté pan over medium heat, add the olive oil. Sauté the onion, tempeh, jalapeño, and garlic for 5 minutes.
2. Pour the tempeh mixture into a 4-quart slow cooker. Add the tomatoes, tomatoes with green chilies, beans, chipotle peppers, and chili powder.
3. Cover and cook on low for 8 hours.
4. In a medium bowl, mix the soymilk, canola oil, baking powder, cornmeal, and salt. Drop ¼-cup mounds in a single layer on top of the tempeh.
5. Cover and cook on high for 20 minutes without lifting the lid. The dumplings will look fluffy and light when fully cooked.

Slow Cooker Suggestions

While fresh tomatoes are delicious, canned tomatoes are a better choice in some recipes because they have already been cooked, and their skins and seeds have been removed. There is also reason to believe that canned tomatoes are better sources of cancer-preventing lycopene simply because they are cooked, and one can of crushed tomatoes or sauce is the equivalent of dozens of fresh tomatoes.

CHAPTER 12

Desserts

Hot Fudge Fondue

YIELDS

4 C

1 cup butter

1 cup heavy cream

½ cup light corn syrup

⅛ teaspoon salt

1 (16-ounce) package semisweet chocolate chips

1 tablespoon vanilla extract

1. Add the butter, cream, corn syrup, and salt to a 4-quart slow cooker. Cover and cook on low for 1 hour.
2. Uncover and stir with a silicone-coated whisk or heatproof spatula; cover and cook for another hour.
3. Uncover and stir or whisk until the salt is completely dissolved.
4. Add the chocolate chips and vanilla. Stir or whisk until the chocolate is completely melted and incorporated into the fondue.
5. Reduce the heat to low until ready to serve directly from the slow cooker.

Chocolate-Cinnamon Fondue

SERVES

16

2 (14-ounce) packages semisweet chocolate chips

2 cups plain soymilk

½ cup butter or vegan margarine

1 tablespoon cinnamon

1. Add all ingredients to a 4-quart slow cooker.
2. Cover and cook on low heat for 1 hour.

Chocolate Cake

2 cups all-purpose flour

2 cups sugar

¾ cup unsweetened cocoa powder

1¾ teaspoons baking powder

1¾ teaspoons baking soda

1¼ cups 2% milk

2 eggs

½ cup vegetable oil

1¼ cups water

1 cup icing

1. In a medium bowl, mix all the dry ingredients.
2. In another medium bowl, mix all the wet ingredients except the icing.
3. Spray a 4-quart slow cooker with nonstick cooking oil.
4. Combine the dry and wet ingredients and pour into the slow cooker.
5. Cover and cook on high heat for 1–2 hours.
6. Remove cake from slow cooker and cover with icing.

White Chocolate–Macadamia Nut Bars

2 (14-ounce) packages white chocolate chips

1 cup macadamia nut pieces

1. Add all ingredients to a 4-quart slow cooker. Cover and cook on low heat for 1 hour, stirring every 15 minutes.
2. With a large spoon, scoop out the white chocolate mixture and drop it onto wax paper. Allow to cool for 20–30 minutes.

Chocolate-Covered Pretzels

SERVES
16

2 (14-ounce) packages semisweet chocolate chips

2 cups plain soymilk

½ cup butter

4 cups miniature pretzels

1. Add all ingredients except pretzels to a 4-quart slow cooker. Cover and cook on low heat for 1 hour.

2. Dip the pretzels in the chocolate and allow to cool on wax paper for 20–30 minutes.

Slow Cooker Suggestions

To easily "dip" all of the pretzels at once, you can drop them all into the finished chocolate sauce in the slow cooker, stir gently, and then pour the entire mixture into a colander to strain the excess chocolate.

Cinnamon Poached Apples

SERVES
8

5 medium apples, peeled, cored, and cut into wedges

3 cups water

1 cup white sugar

1 teaspoon ground ginger

1 teaspoon cinnamon

1. Add all ingredients to a 4-quart slow cooker.

2. Cover and cook on low heat for 4 hours.

Carrot Cake

1½ cups all-purpose flour

½ teaspoon baking soda

1 teaspoon baking powder

¼ teaspoon salt

¾ teaspoon cinnamon

¼ teaspoon ground cloves

⅛ teaspoon freshly grated nutmeg

2 bananas, mashed

¾ cup sugar

⅓ cup Earth Balance Original Buttery Spread

¼ cup water

1 cup grated carrots

½ cup chopped walnuts

1. In a mixing bowl, add the flour, baking soda, baking powder, salt, cinnamon, cloves, and nutmeg. Stir to combine.
2. In a food processor, add the bananas, sugar, and Earth Balance. Process to cream together. Scrape into the flour mixture.
3. Pour in the water and add the grated carrots to the mixing bowl. Stir and fold to combine all ingredients. Fold in the nuts.
4. Treat a 4-quart slow cooker with nonstick spray. Add the carrot cake batter, and use a spatula to spread it evenly in the crock.
5. Cover and cook on low for 2 hours, or until cake is firm in the center.

Peanut Butter Cake

1 cup all-purpose flour

1 cup sugar

1 teaspoon baking powder

$\frac{1}{2}$ teaspoon baking soda

$\frac{3}{4}$ cup water

$\frac{1}{2}$ cup peanut butter

2 tablespoons vegetable oil

1 teaspoon vanilla extract

1. In a medium bowl, mix all the dry ingredients.
2. In another medium bowl, mix all the wet ingredients.
3. Spray slow cooker with nonstick cooking oil.
4. Combine the dry and wet ingredients, and then pour into a 4-quart slow cooker. Cover and cook on high heat for 1–2 hours.

Chocolate Rice Pudding

1 cup white rice

1 quart soymilk

$\frac{1}{2}$ cup Earth Balance Original Buttery Spread

1 cup sugar

$\frac{1}{2}$ cup chocolate syrup

$\frac{1}{4}$ teaspoon salt

1. Add all ingredients to a 4-quart slow cooker.
2. Cover and cook on low heat for 6 hours.

Bananas Foster

1 cup dark corn syrup

2 tablespoons dark rum

½ teaspoon vanilla extract

1 teaspoon cinnamon

¾ cup Earth Balance Original Buttery Spread

¼ teaspoon salt

10 bananas, peeled and cut into bite-sized pieces

4 cups vegan vanilla ice cream

1. In a medium bowl, stir in the corn syrup, rum, vanilla extract, cinnamon, Earth Balance, and salt.
2. Add mixture and bananas to a 4-quart slow cooker.
3. Cover and cook on low heat for 1–2 hours. Serve over a scoop of vegan ice cream.

Date and Nut Bars

1 cup pitted and chopped dates

1 cup cranberries

½ cup almonds

½ cup pecans

1 cup flour

1 cup sugar

1 teaspoon baking powder

¼ cup puréed silken tofu

2 tablespoons Earth Balance Original Buttery Spread

1 teaspoon vanilla extract

1. Combine all of the ingredients in a large mixing bowl, then pour into a 4-quart slow cooker that has been prepared with cooking spray.
2. Cover and cook on high heat for 2 hours.
3. Allow to cool slightly, then cut into small bars. Transfer to a wire rack and allow the bars to cool completely.

Pumpkin Pie

1 (15-ounce) can plain pumpkin

½ cup Bisquick

¼ cup sugar

¼ cup brown sugar

¾ cup soymilk

½ cup puréed silken tofu

2 teaspoons pumpkin pie spice

1 teaspoon vanilla extract

1. Combine all of the ingredients in a large mixing bowl, and then transfer to a 4-quart slow cooker that has been prepared with cooking spray.
2. Cover and cook on low heat for 6 hours.

Chocolate "Mud" Cake

1 cup flour

½ cup sugar

2 teaspoons baking powder

¼ teaspoon salt

3 tablespoons cocoa powder

3 tablespoons softened Earth Balance Original Buttery Spread

1 teaspoon vanilla extract

⅓ cup soymilk

½ cup vegan chocolate chips

1 cup chocolate icing

1. In a large mixing bowl, combine the flour, sugar, baking powder, salt, and cocoa powder.
2. In a medium bowl, combine the Earth Balance, vanilla, and soymilk until well blended.
3. Add the wet mixture and the chocolate chips to the large mixing bowl and stir until just combined.
4. Pour the batter into a greased 4-quart slow cooker.
5. Cover and cook on high heat for 2½ hours.
6. Once done, allow the cake to cool slightly, then top with chocolate icing.

Mixed Berry Cobbler

1 cup flour

¾ cup sugar, divided

1 teaspoon baking powder

¼ teaspoon cinnamon

¼ teaspoon salt

2 eggs

¼ cup puréed silken tofu

1½ cups chopped strawberries

1½ cups raspberries

1 cup blueberries

1 teaspoon lemon juice

1. In a large bowl, combine the flour, ½ cup sugar, baking powder, cinnamon, and salt, then add the eggs and tofu. Stir until well combined.
2. Pour the mixture into a greased 4-quart slow cooker.
3. In a small bowl, combine the remaining ¼ cup sugar, strawberries, raspberries, blueberries, and lemon juice, and then add the berry mixture to the slow cooker.
4. Cover and cook on low for 2½–3 hours.

CHAPTER 13

Sauces

Seitan Marinara

2 tablespoons olive oil

½ medium onion, diced

2 cloves garlic, minced

1 (16-ounce) package seitan, cut into small pieces

2 (14-ounce) cans diced tomatoes

½ teaspoon sugar

1 tablespoon tomato paste

⅓ cup water

1 lemon, juiced

2 tablespoons chopped fresh basil

1 teaspoon salt

¼ teaspoon black pepper

1. Add the olive oil to a skillet and sauté the onion and garlic on medium heat for about 3 minutes.
2. Transfer the onion mixture to a 4-quart slow cooker.
3. Add the rest of the ingredients.
4. Cover and cook on high heat for 2 hours.

Jalapeño-Tomatillo Sauce

1 teaspoon canola oil

2 cloves garlic, minced

1 small onion, sliced

7 tomatillos, diced

2 jalapeños, seeded and minced

½ cup water

1. In a nonstick pan, heat the oil. Add the garlic, onion, tomatillos, and jalapeños and sauté about 5 minutes.
2. In a 4-quart slow cooker, place the mixture; add the water and stir.
3. Cover and cook on low for 8 hours.

Lemon Dill Sauce

SERVES

4

2 cups Vegetable Broth (see recipe in Chapter 4)

½ cup lemon juice

½ cup chopped fresh dill

1 teaspoon salt

¼ teaspoon white pepper

1. In a 2- or 4-quart slow cooker, place all ingredients.
2. Cook on high, uncovered, for 3 hours.

Creamy Dijon Sauce

YIELDS

2 C.

1 tablespoon butter

1 tablespoon flour

1 cup unsweetened soymilk

½ cup white wine

½ cup Vegetable Broth (see recipe in Chapter 4)

2 tablespoons Dijon mustard

¼ cup chopped shallots

½ teaspoon salt

½ teaspoon pepper

1. In a sauté pan, melt the butter over medium heat.
2. Slowly stir in the flour with a whisk and create a roux. Stir in the soymilk and continue whisking until very smooth.
3. Whisk in the white wine and Vegetable Broth and stir until there are no lumps and it is well combined, then pour into a 4-quart slow cooker.
4. Add all remaining ingredients.
5. Cover and cook on low heat for 3 hours.

Country White Gravy

½ cup vegetable oil

¼ cup diced onion

3 cloves garlic, minced

½ cup flour

4 teaspoons nutritional yeast

4 tablespoons soy sauce

2 cups water

½ teaspoon dried sage

½ teaspoon salt

¼ teaspoon pepper

1. In a small saucepan, heat the oil over medium-low heat. Add the onions and garlic and sauté for 2 minutes.
2. Stir in the flour to make a roux, then gradually add the nutritional yeast, soy sauce, and water, stirring constantly.
3. Transfer the mixture to a 4-quart slow cooker on low heat.
4. Add the sage, salt, and pepper, then cover and cook for 1 hour.

Puttanesca Sauce

1 tablespoon olive oil

4 cloves garlic, minced

1 medium onion, diced

1 cup sliced black olives

1 tablespoon olive brine

1 (28 ounce) can crushed tomatoes

1 (15-ounce) can diced tomatoes

1 tablespoon red pepper flakes

2 tablespoons drained nonpareil capers

2 tablespoons chopped fresh basil

1. In a large sauté pan, heat the olive oil over medium heat. Add the garlic and onion and sauté until soft, 3–4 minutes.
2. In a 4-quart slow cooker, place the onions and garlic; add the remaining ingredients. Stir to distribute the ingredients evenly.
3. Cook on low for 4–6 hours. If the sauce looks very wet at the end of the cooking time, remove the lid and cook on high for 15–30 minutes before serving.

White Wine–Garlic Sauce

6 tablespoons butter

2 tablespoons minced shallot

5 cloves garlic, minced

1 cup white wine

1 cup Vegetable Broth (see recipe in Chapter 4)

1½ teaspoons salt

1. In a sauté pan, melt the butter over medium heat. Add the shallot and garlic and sauté for 2 minutes.
2. Add the sautéed blend to a 4-quart slow cooker.
3. Add all remaining ingredients, stir, and cook on low for 2 hours.

Three-Pepper Sauce

1 (28-ounce) can diced tomatoes

2 tablespoons tomato paste

1 red bell pepper, seeded and finely diced

1 green bell pepper, seeded and finely diced

½ medium red onion, diced

3 cloves garlic, minced

1 teaspoon cayenne pepper

½ teaspoon sugar

½ teaspoon salt

1. In a 4-quart slow cooker, add all ingredients.
2. Cover and cook on low heat for 6–8 hours.

Red Pepper Coulis

2 tablespoons olive oil

2 shallots, minced

2 red bell peppers, seeded and diced

2 cloves garlic, minced

1 cup Vegetable Broth (see recipe in Chapter 4)

¼ cup plain unsweetened soymilk

¼ teaspoon salt

⅛ teaspoon black pepper

1. Add the oil to a sauté pan and sauté the shallots and red peppers on medium-high heat for 3–5 minutes.
2. Add the garlic and sauté for 1 minute more, then add to a 4-quart slow cooker.
3. Add the rest of the ingredients and cook on high heat for 2 hours.

Sun-Dried Tomato Sauce

¼ cup Earth Balance Original Buttery Spread

¼ cup white flour

3½ cups plain unsweetened soymilk

1 cup chopped sun-dried tomatoes

1 tablespoon vegan Worcestershire sauce

1 teaspoon salt

¼ teaspoon black pepper

1. In a sauté pan, melt the Earth Balance over medium heat. Slowly stir in the flour with a whisk and create a roux.
2. Stir in the soymilk and continue whisking until very smooth.
3. Add the roux and the rest of the ingredients to a 2-quart slow cooker and cook on low heat for 2 hours, stirring occasionally.

Red Wine Reduction

2 tablespoons olive oil

1 shallot, minced

2 cloves garlic, minced

1 cup red wine

1 cup Vegetable Broth (see recipe in Chapter 4)

¼ cup Earth Balance Original Buttery Spread

1. Add the oil to a sauté pan and sauté the shallot on medium-high heat for 3 minutes.

2. Add the garlic and sauté for 1 minute more, then add to a 4-quart slow cooker.

3. Add the remaining ingredients and cook on high heat until the sauce has reduced by half, approximately 1–2 hours.

Slow-Roasted Garlic and Tomato Sauce

2 tablespoons olive oil

2½ pounds fresh, vine-ripened tomatoes, peeled and diced

1 teaspoon dried parsley

1 teaspoon dried basil

1 tablespoon balsamic vinegar

½ teaspoon granulated cane sugar

¼ teaspoon salt

¼ teaspoon black pepper

3 heads roasted garlic, cloves removed from peel

1. Add all ingredients to a 4-quart slow cooker.
2. Cover and cook on low for 3–4 hours.

Slow Cooker Suggestions

Roast whole heads of garlic by cutting off the top quarter, drizzling with olive oil, and then wrapping in aluminum foil. Cook in an oven preheated to 400°F for about 45 minutes.

Easy Peanut Sauce

1 cup creamy peanut butter

4 tablespoons maple syrup

½ cup sesame oil

1 teaspoon cayenne pepper

1½ teaspoons cumin

1 teaspoon garlic powder

1½ teaspoons salt

2 cups water

1. In a blender, add all ingredients except for the water.
2. Blend as you slowly add the water until you reach the desired consistency.
3. Pour the sauce into a 2-quart slow cooker and cook on low heat for 1 hour.

Coconut Curry Sauce

1 (14-ounce) can coconut milk

1 cup Vegetable Broth (see recipe in Chapter 4)

1 teaspoon soy sauce

1 tablespoon curry paste

1 tablespoon lime juice

2 cloves garlic, minced

½ teaspoon salt

¼ cup chopped fresh cilantro

1. In a 4-quart slow cooker, add all ingredients except cilantro.
2. Cover and cook on low heat for 2 hours.
3. Add the chopped cilantro and cook for an additional 30 minutes.

Mole

2 tablespoons olive oil

½ small onion, finely diced

3 cloves garlic, minced

1 teaspoon cumin

¼ teaspoon cinnamon

¼ teaspoon coriander

1 tablespoon chili powder

2 chipotle peppers in adobo, seeded and minced

1 teaspoon salt

4 cups Vegetable Broth (see recipe in Chapter 4)

1 ounce vegan dark chocolate, chopped

1. In a sauté pan over medium heat, add the oil, onion, and garlic, and sauté about 3 minutes.
2. Add the cumin, cinnamon, and coriander, and sauté for 1 minute.
3. Transfer the sautéed mixture to a 4-quart slow cooker.
4. Add the chili powder, chipotles, and salt, then whisk in the Vegetable Broth. Finally, add the chocolate.
5. Cover and cook on high heat for 2 hours.

US/Metric Conversion Chart

VOLUME CONVERSIONS

US Volume Measure	Metric Equivalent
⅛ teaspoon	0.5 milliliter
¼ teaspoon	1 milliliter
½ teaspoon	2 milliliters
1 teaspoon	5 milliliters
½ tablespoon	7 milliliters
1 tablespoon (3 teaspoons)	15 milliliters
2 tablespoons (1 fluid ounce)	30 milliliters
¼ cup (4 tablespoons)	60 milliliters
⅓ cup	90 milliliters
½ cup (4 fluid ounces)	125 milliliters
⅔ cup	160 milliliters
¾ cup (6 fluid ounces)	180 milliliters
1 cup (16 tablespoons)	250 milliliters
1 pint (2 cups)	500 milliliters
1 quart (4 cups)	1 liter (about)

WEIGHT CONVERSIONS

US Weight Measure	Metric Equivalent
½ ounce	15 grams
1 ounce	30 grams
2 ounces	60 grams
3 ounces	85 grams
¼ pound (4 ounces)	115 grams
½ pound (8 ounces)	225 grams
¾ pound (12 ounces)	340 grams
1 pound (16 ounces)	454 grams

OVEN TEMPERATURE CONVERSIONS

Degrees Fahrenheit	Degrees Celsius
200 degrees F	95 degrees C
250 degrees F	120 degrees C
275 degrees F	135 degrees C
300 degrees F	150 degrees C
325 degrees F	160 degrees C
350 degrees F	180 degrees C
375 degrees F	190 degrees C
400 degrees F	205 degrees C
425 degrees F	220 degrees C
450 degrees F	230 degrees C

BAKING PAN SIZES

American	Metric
8 x 1½ inch round baking pan	20 x 4 cm cake tin
9 x 1½ inch round baking pan	23 x 3.5 cm cake tin
11 x 7 x 1½ inch baking pan	28 x 18 x 4 cm baking tin
13 x 9 x 2 inch baking pan	30 x 20 x 5 cm baking tin
2 quart rectangular baking dish	30 x 20 x 3 cm baking tin
15 x 10 x 2 inch baking pan	30 x 25 x 2 cm baking tin (Swiss roll tin)
9 inch pie plate	22 x 4 or 23 x 4 cm pie plate
7 or 8 inch springform pan	18 or 20 cm springform or loose bottom cake tin
9 x 5 x 3 inch loaf pan	23 x 13 x 7 cm or 2 lb narrow loaf or pate tin
1½ quart casserole	1.5 liter casserole
2 quart casserole	2 liter casserole

INDEX

INDEX

Note: Page numbers in **bold** indicate recipe category lists.